MARCO ⊕ POLO

Travel with
Insider Tips

VENICE

GERMANY
FL   **AUSTRIA**
   Innsbruck
SWITZER-
LAND   Bolzano   **SLOVENIA**
   Venice
   Milan   **CROATIA**
   Genoa   **BOSNIA-**
   ITALY   **HERZEGOVINA**
Gulf of
Genoa   Ancona
   SAN
Corsica   **MARINO**   Adriatic
(F)   Sea
   Rome

www.marco-polo.com

SYMBOLS

INSIDERTIP	Insider Tip
★	Highlight
●●●●	Best of...
☼	Scenic view
⊕	Responsible travel: for ecological or fair trade aspects
(*)	Telephone numbers that are not toll-free

**PRICE CATEGORIES
HOTELS**

Expensive	over 190 euros
Moderate	115–190 euros
Budget	under 115 Euro

Average prices for the cheapest double room. There can be huge variations in price – in both directions – depending on the season

**PRICE CATEGORIES
RESTAURANTS**

Expensive	over 45 euros
Moderate	20–45 euros
Budget	under 20 euros

Price for a threecourse meal, typical for the particular restaurant, without drinks

DID YOU KNOW?
Books & films → p. 24
Relax & enjoy → p. 32
The Vogalonga rowing event → p. 44
Gourmet restaurants → p. 65
Local specialities → p. 68
Luxury hotels → p. 86
National holidays → p. 105
Budgeting → p. 109
Keep fit! → p. 111
Weather → p. 112
Currency converter → p. 113

MAPS IN THE GUIDEBOOK
(120 A1) Page numbers and coordinates refer to the street atlas and the regional map on p. 130/131
(O) Site/address located off the map

Coordinates are also given for places that are not marked on the street atlas

(🕮 A–B 2–3) refers to the removable pull-out map
(🕮 O) Site/address located of the map

FRONT COVER:
The best Highlights

BACK COVER:
Plan of the *vaporetto* lines

The best MARCO POLO Insider Tips

Our top 15 Insider Tips

INSIDER TIP **Charming views**
Whether a morning stroll or festive evening reception, rowing regatta, ball game, funeral or procession of penitents: the picture gallery in the delightful *Museo Querini Stampalia* throws light on Venetian everyday life in the 18th century → **p. 43**

INSIDER TIP **Little-known Tintorettos**
The Gothic *Madonna dell'Orto* church is the home of an exquisite collection of paintings, including several by Tintoretto → **p. 48**

INSIDER TIP **A charitable feast**
At the youthful and inviting restaurant *Fantàsia,* run by a charity organization, you can enjoy pizzas, pasta dishes or fish specialities while also helping those suffering from rare diseases or other handicaps → **p. 69**

INSIDER TIP **There's no place like home!**
Giuseppe Galardi's Osteria *Al Assassini* serves up daily specials *alla casa* → **p. 63**

INSIDER TIP **Model ships as souvenirs**
From fret saw kits for children to painstakingly detailed replicas of large sailing ships and galleys that have taken hundreds of hours of work: *Gilberto Penzo* creates fascinating boats and ships en miniature in his workshop → **p. 75**

INSIDER TIP **Dining on Murano**
For creative cuisine and excellent wines, head to *Vecchia Pescheria* in a stylishly renovated old factory and its idyllic terrace → **p. 67**

INSIDER TIP **Smart slip-ons**
Cooler than the coolest flip-flops: the non-slip, velvety-soft shoes worn by the gondolieri in *Piedàterre* → **p. 75**

INSIDER TIP **Music lovers, take note!**
Operas in historic costumes are staged in the lovely *Scuola Grande dei Carmini* → **p. 53**

BEST OF...

FOR FREE

● *San Marco – the treasure chest*
Admission to the grand, richly ornamented *St Mark's Basilica*, this orgy of gold, silver and precious stones, is free -- not only that, but from spring to autumn, guided tours to the gorgeous stone mosaics don't cost anything either → p. 33, 36

● *Tête-à-Tête with death*
What do the composer Igor Stravinsky, the poet Ezra Pound and the dancer Sergei Diaghilev have in common? They and many other famous people have found their final resting place o the cemetery island *San Michele*. Visit their graves and be captured by the atmosphere of this freely accessible site (photo) → p. 57

● *Partying under the stars*
Chatting with the locals while enjoying a glass of wine is easy, weather permitting, as many of the squares turn into proper open-air party venues where you don't have to buy drinks. Some of the most popular spots are the Campi *Santa Margherita* and *San Bartolomeo* → p. 80

● *Museum of harmony*
Listen to the hits of days long gone as Baroque music fills the air while you explore the exhibition of well-crafted flutes, violas, violins and lutes in the church of *San Maurizio* in the heart of San Marco → p. 36

● *Superlative painting*
What is supposedly the largest Baroque ceiling painting in the world is hidden behind the modest brick façade of *San Pantalon* church – a colossal work put together out of 40 individual canvas elements, freely accessible → p. 57

● *Stroll through luxurious film sets*
The *Grand Hotel des Bains* on the Lido served as the backdrop for Luchino Visconti's world-famous film adaptation of Thomas Mann's "Death in Venice". The terrace, foyer, restaurants and park still exude this glamorous aura of the past and can be toured discreetly without having to pay a cent → p. 58

◗ ◖ ◗ ◖ ◗ ● Dots in guidebook refer to "Best of..." tips

ONLY IN VENICE
Unique experiences

● *Floating icons of the city*
Many visitors feel that a ride in a *gondola* is the epitome of romance. Anybody who has ever glided over the waters of the peaceful canals will understand why (photo) → p. 110

● *Sundowner or dinner at the Rialto*
The district on the *bank of the Canal Grande* between the fish market and Fabbriche Vecchie has the reputation of being a really trendy place. You will understand why if you feast on, or sip, the specialties served at one of the tables in the open air → p. 76

● *Lively festivals*
The Venetian carnival is known around the world. But, the Venetians also demonstrate their talent for celebrating at several smaller festivals worth attending throughout the year, including the *Asparagus Festival* in Cavallino, the *Fishermen's Festival of Malamocco* and the *Wine Festival on Sant'Erasmo* → p. 104, 105

● *The island of the lacemakers*
For centuries, Venetian lace has been known for its quality. If you visit the little picturesque island of *Burano,* you can learn how lace is made at one of the needlepoint schools and admire pieces sewn by local craftspeople in the museum → p. 57

● *Bellini, Titian, Tintoretto & Co.*
From momentous Biblical scenes by the great masters of the Renaissance to the genre and landscape paintings of the Baroque and Rococo periods: nowhere else can art lovers find such a wealth from the quintessence of Venetian painting of this quality than in the *Galleria dell'Accademia* → p. 54

● *The whole city turned into a masked ball*
Every year, the Venetians revel in a feast for all the senses at the *classic carnival* (Mardi Gras) from the middle of January to Shrove Tuesday – the best time to let yourself be enchanted by Venice! → p. 104

● *Long promenade on the waterside*
When there is still snow on the mainland, the first sunrays of spring tickle the skin on the *Zattere* in Dorsoduro. But a walk along the quay with a view over the Giudecca Canal is sure to warm your heart → p. 52

ONLY IN

9

BEST OF...

● Discover the Doge's palace

For almost 1,000 years, 120 doges determined the fate of the Sea Republic from this gigantic complex of buildings. It is no wonder that the halls are so elaborately decorated (photo) → p. 39

● Flying visit in style

Coffee and cake in the lobby of *Danieli*: you will feel like you have been transported back to the 15th century in the covered courtyard of this Gothic palace with its marble arches and balustrades, silk tapestries and oriental carpets – not only on rainy days → p. 86

● Make your own mask

They are one of the features of the Carnival in Venice: the artistic masks the costumed people wear. At *Ca' Macana*, you can not only buy one of these works of art but also spend a couple of hours learning how to make one → p. 74

● The maritime heritage of St Mark's Republic

Housed in an old warehouse in the Arsenal wharf area, the *Museo Storico Navale* brings back memories of the glorious times at sea through documents, instruments and – above all – hundreds of magnificent models of ships. Also fascinating for the children! → p. 43

● Place your bets!

If it rains, you can spend a few hours in the noble atmosphere of Richard Wagner's final home playing roulette, blackjack or poker. The *Casino* is located in a magnificent Renaissance palace → p. 78

● Art of the 20th century

Modern art is a welcome change in a city that can look back over 500 years of painting. You will find works by all of the great masters of 20th century art in the *Collezione Peggy Guggenheim* → p. 53

RAIN

RELAX AND CHILL OUT
Take it easy and spoil yourself

● *A drink in a fairy-tale setting*
The terraces of famous hotels such as the *Monaco & Grand Canal* are the perfect places for a *spritz* or glass of *spumante* – lean back and enjoy the service → **p. 84**

● *Relax with music*
Monteverdi, Vivaldi, Albinoni: the ensemble *Interpreti Veneziani* offers a fine opportunity to hear works by the great masters of Renaissance and Baroque music. They give more than 200 concerts a year in the former San Vidal Church → **p. 78**

● *A green oasis to get your energy back*
The monks of *The St Regis Venice San Clemente Palace* on the island of the same name would be astonished to see what their monastery has developed into: a luxury hotel with spa facilities, open-air pool and spacious park. A wonderful place to unwind, and only ten minutes by boat from the hustle and bustle of the city → **p. 86**

● *Chill out in style*
At the moment, two of the hottest addresses for the trend-setting international crowd are *Tarnowska's American Bar* and the *B-Bar* at the luxury hotel Bauer's. Especially at the latter one, you have a real chance to meet a world-famous star → **p. 79, 80**

● *Take a dip at the Lido*
A day (or at least half a day) on the sandy beach at the *Lido* makes a welcome change from exploring the labyrinthine old city. You will be able to get your breath back relaxing in a deck chair or swimming in the Adriatic Sea (photo)
→ **p. 102**

● *Take a break in a green oasis*
Need to recover from sightseeing? A perfect place to do this is under the cypress trees in the g*arden of the church of San Francesco della Vigna.* It is one of the green oases that the Venetians are now starting to rediscover → **p. 19**

INTRODUCTION

DISCOVER VENICE!

Nobody arriving in Venice for the first time can really claim never to have seen this "Wonder of the World" before: It has been described, sung about, shown in pictures and films so often that it has long made its way into the collective consciousness of Europe as a whole. The *palaces on the main canals with water lapping around them* really look just as opulent and crumbling at the same time as they do in opulent coffee-table books and travel brochures. The Piazza San Marco with the basilica of the same name at one end is as chic and perfect in reality as it appears on film sets. And the panorama from the quay in front of the Doge's Palace across the water towards San Giorgio and Giudecca is exactly the same, down to the tiniest details, as the one Canaletto painted.

But after only walking for an hour or two through the *labyrinth of small streets, squares and back courtyards* you will start to realise that you are discovering much more than simply an architecturally city of exceptional beauty with more priceless art treasures than any other. No, here you will understand that it is necessary to try to capture the feeling of what is possibly the most wondrous city in the world with all your senses and, hopefully, at your leisure.

Photo: A cruise ship docked before San Giorgio Maggiore

The wonder started to develop in 500 AD when people from the mainland, the Veneti, fled to the lagoon to escape from the Huns and Lombards. Shortly after 800, they began connecting dozens of small islands with bridges and drove millions of wooden piles into the muddy ground to create the 7.5 km² city area that we know today with its 3,000 lanes and 100 squares, around 150 canals and *more than 400 bridges*.

Newcomers can get a first impression of the *unique location* and layout of this city from a church tower. For example, you have a wonderful view of the outline of the city from the Campanile of the Benedictine monastery San Giorgio Maggiore. To the east, you will see the huge area of the Arsenal, the shipyards. A little further to the east, the green of the Giardini Pubblici, the city park, and the neighbouring Biennale exhibition area beckons a visit. The concrete carparks and railway station rise up above the rust-red roofs in the west and you will be able to make out the chimneys of the factories in Maghera and Mestre belching smoke into the – all-too-often smoggy – sky in the distance. On the other hand, you will almost be able to reach out and touch the large, reversed "S" of the Canal Grande.

> **The most amazing urban settlement on earth**

A total of six districts – the so-called "Sixths" (Italian: *sestieri*) – form the historical city centre *(centro storico)* and are surrounded by dozens of islands. Some of them are

Carnival is not the only festival celebrated on the streets of Venice: Festa del Redentore in July

still used for specific purposes – San Michele, for example, is the cemetery island, and Sant'Erasmo and Le Vignole the vegetable islands. Not to forget the *glassblowers' island of Murano* and the old episcopal see of Torcello with Burano, the lacemakers' haven, in between, and the *Lido*, the narrow sandy promontory between the lagoon and open sea on the southern horizon.

More than 25 million visitors from all over the world descend on this urban miracle every year and the contrasting feelings it produces give you an idea of how multi-faceted it is. On the one hand, it is *melancholy and decadent*. You cannot help but think of the lugubrious verses penned by Lord Byron and other poets of his age, the immortal thrillers such as the chill of

> **The melancholic, morbid atmosphere can be felt everywhere**

the city described in Patricia Highsmith's "Those Who Walk Away", Daphne du Maurier's funereal gondolas in "Don't Look Now", Thomas Mann's novel "Death in Venice" and Luchino Visconti's filmed version, and of course Donna Leon's Commissario Brunetti. Venice's potency in matters of love is closely linked to its often alluded to *tristezza*. Desdemona and Othello, George Sand and Alfred de Musset and, of course, tireless Giacomo Casanova all represent the – often tragic – *passions* this dream city can arouse. On the other hand, Venice's mastery in *celebrating exuberant festivitites* stands in complete contrast to all this gloominess and can still be observed today during the carnival season and in the many gloriously colourful regattas held in the middle of summer for the Redentore feast day.

In a manner of speaking, the biological situation of the city is also inconsistent: it is no secret that Venice is noticeably aging. Both demographically and in terms of the city itself: it has sunk more than 10 cm in 20 years; its *buildings are crumbling*, shaken day and night by the gigantic engines of an ever increasing number of enormous cruise liners that have sailed closer and closer to the historic palaces and piazzas over the years. Although the Venetians pushed through a city-wide prohibition against these ocean-going giants after years of debate in 2014, a court has since overturned this decision. It still remains unclear how this problem will be dealt with in the future.

In the 1950s, 175,000 people lived in the city; this has decreased to a third of that figure today. And more than a third of these almost *60,000 reminaing residents* go to work every day on the mainland. What is the reason for this exodus, the *esodo*? After 1945, the cramped living conditions, damp walls and lack of leisure activities were problems that caused young families to leave Venice and move into new, more comfortable, artificially created settlements in the Mestre area. And then, the stream of visitors that started to inundate the city when mass tourism set in with such vehemence in the 1970s washed even more of the locals out of the lagoon.

Many people forget how arduous it is to live in this city that the masses are now threatening to suffocate completely. The *vaporetti* and main streets are hopelessly overcrowded during peak times. And, everyday life is really quite difficult. Within a generation, the number of retail shops has decreased by more than 50 percent. In many districts, if the Venetians want to pop out to buy bread and milk, this can mean a long walk over countless bridges – especially tiresome for old people. All essential goods have to be laboriously brought into the city on barges and then hauled up flights of steps on a sack barrow. The demands of well-heeled tourists have made life unaffordable for many of locals earning average wages. The *costs for cosumer articles*, as well as council taxes, are out of control. Another major problem is that wealthy foreigners are purchasing empty flats as second homes causing property prices to rocket – taking rents with them.

> **The Venetians are masters at staging exuberant festivals**

This has caused the population pyramid to become inverted. Today, there are almost five times as many Venetians over 60 than under 20 years of age. Along with this, more recently, a lively nightlife and cabaret scene has developed, especially in Dorsoduro and Cannaregio that has remained almost unnoticed by the world outside the lagoon. This now attracts *hordes of young night-owls thirsty for adventure*, among them thousands of guest students from the local university.

Venice has always been able to come to grips with any circumstances. The Venetians have been gifted merchants since time immemorial; this was the case in 1204 when, under the leadership of the 97-year-old, completely blind, Doge Enrico Dandolo, they simply diverted the Fourth Crusade to Constantinople and plundered the treasures of their fellow Christians there. And that is how it continued during the following centuries when *the doges* safeguarded the internal and external interests of the Republic with a rod of iron and Venice raked in unbelievable sums of money as the dominant trading nation in the Eastern Mediterranean.

When the Venetians lost their first foreign possessions in the 14th century, they started to turn their eyes towards the *terra firma*. Shortly after 1400, Venice conquered Istria, Friuli, Vicenza, Verona and Padua, as well as large sections of Lombardy and used them to provide wood for its fleet, grain and vegetables for its kitchens, and fabric and silk for its festivals.

The tide has turned in recent decades. Formally, Venice is still the capital of the Veneto but the region's heart now beats in boom towns on the mainland. Their flagships are Benetton (in Ponzano near Treviso), Stefanel (Ponte di Piave) and Eni (Marghera). All the plans to unite this area of concentrated industry — where around 2.5 million people live and 1 million work — to form a dynamic

A lively restaurant and cabaret scene

metropolis and establish a major harbour near Chioggia that could play an important role in Central Europe have been flogged to death without anything coming of them.

The gondola pier at San Marco is only this empty during the (very) early morning hours

However, the advocates of a romantic image of Venice will be really pleased about the city on the lagoon's inability to benefit from the progress in its surroundings — something that many criticise. It is precisely the *special character of this island people* that they enjoy so much: their proud, but somewhat diffident temperament, the strangely melancholic dialect and the years of old-fashioned aversion to the automobile now seem to be really avant-garde.

WHAT'S HOT

1 Creative hotbed

Dorsoduro The hotspot for creative people is in the southwest of the city. Dorsoduro is not only where the major galleries are to be found but also hidden gems such as the *Galleria d'Arte l'Occhio (Calle del Bastion 181–85 | www.gallerialocchio.net | photo)*. Local artists like Lalla Malvezzi and Ettore Greco organise exhibitions in this district; for example, in the picturesque *Bac Art Studios (Campo San Vio 862, www.bacart.com)*. Art and cool drinks are on the menu of the first café gallery in the district, the *Imagina Café (Campo Santa Margherita 3126 | www. imaginacafe.it)*. Fascinating works on the walls and animated discussions are guaranteed.

Sporty views

Paddling and dancing Discover Venice from a vertical position! Wanda Moretti will show you how vertical dancing is performed on the facades of houses and even provide instruction *(Piazzale Roma 468b | www. ilposto.org)*. Alternatively, you can get to know the city from the water – at your own speed, in a kayak: *Venice Kayak (Via Servi di Maria 41 | www.venicekayak.com | photo)*.

3 Cabaret revival

A genre has conquered Venice Cabaret and comedy are experiencing a revival in the city. *Carlo e Giorgio (www.carloegiorgio.it | photo)* are master entertainers. Among the many places the two cabaret artists perform are the *Teatro Aurora (Via Padre Egidio Gelain 11 | Marghera)* and the *Teatro Goldoni (Corte Teatro 4650b | www.tea trostabileveneto.it)* where the theatrical heartbeat of the city is at its strongest.

Green Venice

4

Not only water The Venetians have started to re-discover the treasures of their green gardens – and are making them accessible to tourists. Gardens of hotels and monasteries and even private plots hidden behind high walls which are normally closed the the public are opening their doors for you. You can visit the absolutely non-touristy *Parco Savorgnàn (Canale di Cannaregio)* with its old laurel trees, and the mature trees in the small *Parco Villa Groggia (Fondamenta dei Reformati)* on your own. The ● garden of *San Francesco della Vigna church (Campo San Francesco della Vigna)* is a green oasis and a wonderful place to relax in the shade of its cypresses after a busy day sightseeing.

Keeping with the times

5

Contemporary art If you are ready to leave the magnificent legacy of the Gothic, Renaissance and Baroque eras behind and step into the present-day, then the many interesting galleries around La Serenissima are just the thing. For example, in San Marco, you can head to: *La Galleria Van der Koelen (Calle Calegheri 2566),* whose German owners focus on bringing international avant-garde art into the lagoon; *Galleria Traghetto (Campo Santa Maria del Giglio 2543),* which specializes in niche styles; *Jarach Gallery (Campo San Fantin 1997),* which is the best address for contemporary photography; and *Caterina Tognon Arte Contemporanea (Calle del Dose 2746 | photo),* which hosts solo exhibitions by established as well as up-and-coming artists.

IN A NUTSHELL

ACQUA ALTA

Today, the Venetians are still unable to forget what happened that day: The sirocco, the stormy south-east wind, started to blow in the afternoon and drive the waters of the Adriatic into the lagoon. A few hours later, the water-level was almost 6½ feet above normal. The water on Piazza San Marco had never been as high before. Since that notorious day, 4 November 1966, at the latest, Venice's sinking no longer appears to be just a romantic vision but a real threat. Help came from Rome, as well as from private individuals and organisations, in the form of money for reconstruction work. But the water continues to rise. In the past 20 years, the sirens have warned against *acqua alta*, high water, almost 100 times – 5 times more often than in the entire century before. Industrial complexes on the mainland have pumped off ground water, channels have been dredged out for oil tankers and the up-keep of the foundations of the buildings in Venice is poor; all of these have come at a cost.

It is hoped that a colossal project will be able to alleviate this permanently. An industrial syndicate named Venezia Nuova has been working on this plan since the mid-1980s. The Modello Sperimentale Elettromeccanico (MOSE) is a system of 70 gigantic steel flood-gates, hollow bodies 15 m (49 ft) high and 20 m (66 ft) wide, installed in the entrances to the harbours at the Lido, Malamoccco and Chioggia that will be

Photo: Flood waters on Piazza San Marco

Marco Polo, carnival and doges: what you need to know to understand the floating city and plan a perfect holiday

automatically raised by compressed air if the water level rises 3½ ft above normal. This mammoth project was hampered for years as a result of a lack of money and protests from environmental organisations, but it has been "full steam ahead" since 2003. The "Moses" system (from the abbreviation in Italian) designed to protect Venice against dangerous floods finally began operating in 2014. A few photo impressions of the "flooded city" of Venice are available for example at *www.telegraph.co.uk/travel/picturegalleries/9648997/Venice-underwater-during-high-tide-flooding.html*.

BRIDGES TO THE MAINLAND

In 1840, the Habsburg Emperor Ferdinand I authorised the construction of a train link between Venice and Milan with a railway bridge connecting the mainland with the *centro storico*. When the more than 3 km (1.9 miles) long bridge with its 222 arches was solemnly opened in 1846, Venice's existence as an island in the lagoon and in time came to an end and it found itself in the modern age. Unforeseen numbers of tourists began to pour from the station over the bridges through the newly laid out Strada Nuova into the city; commerce and production experienced a boom period. In 1884, the Venetians finally overcame another of their deep-seated fears of being dependent on the mainland: they built the aqueduct that still brings 64 million m³ (17 million gal) of drinking water into the city on the lagoon from the mountains. And finally, the road bridge, Ponte della Libertà, was built parallel to the railway embankment in the period between World War I and World War II. It was expanded in 2015 to accommodate a tram line connecting Mestre and Venice.

C ARNIVAL

The city on the lagoon turns into a fairy-tale land in the last one and a half weeks before Lent when tens of thousands of people wander through Venice in their imaginative robes and its streets and squares become peopled by all the characters from the *commedia dell'arte*. For centuries, this masquerading made it possible for Venetians to escape the watchful eye of the state for a short time at least. The occupier Napoleon, however, was suspicious and thought that conspiracy could flourish behind the masks and completely forbid the masquerade. It was not reintroduced until 1979.

Since then, hoteliers, restaurant owners and sponsors rub their hands in glee when hosts of people from all over the world, craving fun and masquerading, make their way to the city every year in what used to be the off-season in winter to pose, promenade around the city and, if their finances allow it, throw private parties in rented palaces. And, although very few locals mingle with the masses, and the number of spectators and paparazzi probably far exceed those in disguise, (and although awful Mickey Mouse, King Kong and Maya the Bee masks can be seen among the classical costumes), everybody agrees that taking part and the unique atmosphere still compensate for the trip and the often drastically increased room rates.

D IALECT

Between themselves, the Venetians speak the dialect they have used since time immemorial as a sign of their self-esteem. In some aspects, it is similar to Spanish and follows its own rules not only in terms of pronunciation but also in spelling and grammar. The people who live on the lagoon love to contract long (place) names. For example, San Zanipolo is an abbreviated form of the famous church of Santi Giovanni e Paolo, and San Zan Degola (John the Beheaded) is San Giovanni Decolato. Other characteristics: many consonants are voiced; a typical case is *amico* that turns into the Spanish-sounding *amigo*. In Venetian a sharp "s" often takes the place of the Italian *ch* and *sh* sounds – *cento* is pronounced *sento*. And, "z" often becomes an "x". A classic example is one you will notice on advertisements for many trattorias: *cucina venexiana.*

D OGES

Were these men really to be envied? As a doge, they took on the highest office the most powerful city state on earth had to offer and were then not allowed to leave the Republic without permission. They were neither allowed to choose their advisors themselves nor receive emissaries in private. Accepting gifts was just as forbidden as going to a café or theatre let alone abdicating of their own accord. They were not even allowed to write letters to their wives without it passing through the censor's hands. And, after the 11th century, they didn't even have any real power. Starting in 697, they reigned high-handedly and autonomously as medieval sovereigns. They negotiated with emperors and popes, decided on war or peace independently what had once been such a prestigious office.

GONDOLAS

They are a little over 10 metres (almost 33 feet) long and almost 1.5 metres (just about 5 feet) wide, weigh 350 kg (770 lbs) empty, and consist of a total of 280 individual elements including the walnut oarlock *(forcola)* and seven-pronged iron prow *(ferro)* that weighs

When the *gondolieri* take a break: Venetian still-life

and even named their own successor. However, in 1032, a doge fell victim to his own lust for power and his attempts to institute a hereditary character for the office. In a flash, both he and his son were assassinated and the authority of his successors radically restricted. Degraded to simple executive officers, they were placed under the surveillance of the infamous Council of the Ten, a kind of medieval state security service. In later years this led to hardly any halfway capable person being prepared to accept

20 kg (44 lbs). It is estimated that around 10,000 gondolas were in operation on Venice's canals in the 16th century. Today, only about 400 gondolieri are still active. However, there can be no talk about an end coming to the gondola business. Thanks to the trade being passed on within the family, there is no difficulty in finding recruits and, in spite of five months of slow business in the off season, also no financial problems. The order books of the *squeri* – the gondola shipyards – the most photogenic of

which can be visited on Campo San Trovaso not far from the Zattere –, are full for years to come. A newly built boat, painted in traditional black, will set the new owner back about 15,000 euros (13,000 pounds).

LION OF ST MARK

No, the Venetians were not the only people to take the lion as their heraldic animal. But nobody else gave the king of the beasts two wings and placed a book between its front paws. There are different explanations of why this strange hybrid creature should represent Saint Mark of all people. Today, the number (and number of different forms) of the stone big cat are bewildering. You will see the Lion of Saint Mark on façades, cornices and capitals, on chimneys, graves, flowerpots, paintings, and statues of him out in the open.

MARCO POLO

Of course, he deserves special mention in a guidebook that is named after him seeing that Marco Polo, who was born in Venice in 1254 and died there 70 years later, is still considered the epitome of the (world) traveller driven by a yearning to see distant places and a thirst for knowledge. The merchant's son was only an adolescent when he set out across the Adriatic on his way to Asia; he spent many years in China and only returned by sea to the lagoon 24 years later. In Genoese custody, he later dictated his travel report *Il Milione* to a fellow prisoner; it became a bestseller in the Middle Ages and played a decisive role in shaping the Europeans' geographical notion of Asia. The Polo family's house was located not far from Rialto Bridge where the Teatro Malibran stands today.

BOOKS & FILMS

Don't Look Now – Crime writers are especially inspired by the unique, melancholy atmosphere: Daphne du Maurier set her short story, which was later sensitively filmed by Nicholas Roeg, in Venice

Those Who Walk Away – Patricia Highsmith's thriller also takes place in the floating city

Commissario Brunetti – An essential companion for visitors to Venice; the Venetian-by-choice Donna Leon has written 24 crime stories featuring the police commissioner – so far

No Fixed Abode – The two authors Carlo Fruttero and Franco Lucentini wove an especially charming love and crime story around the melancholy Venetian Mr Silvera

Death in Venice – Unadulterated melancholy characterises Thomas Mann's legendary novella. Luchino Visconti's film (1971) is one of the all-time classics

Don Giovanni – Venice plays a picturesque main role in Joseph Losey's adaptation of Mozart's opera as well as in Federico Fellini's film *Casanova* (1976)

POVEGLIA

The waters around Venice's *centro storico* are sprinkled with little islands, many of which have a quite special history. Poveglia's former uses are particularly interesting. This island in front of the Lido in the south of the lagoon near Malamocco may only measure 17.3 acres, but it was once a sanctuary for deposed doges, a quarantine station when epidemics raged, and even a satellite municipal home for the aged and infirm. In the 20th century, however, the island along with its few desolate buildings, vineyards and fruit trees fell into a deep sleep. It was unexpectedly awakened from its slumber in 2014 when the Italian government decided to quickly privatize a number of prime pieces of real estate to help alleviate its major budget deficit. The jewel in the crown, so to speak, was to be the island of Poveglia – the last open patch of land in the lagoon city. But, a group of strong-minded Venetians decided to put a spoke in the government's plans because they did not like the idea that another island would be transformed into a luxury resort by a well-heeled hotel chain. Under the motto *Poveglia per tutti* (Poveglia for all), they launched a Facebook campaign to encourage their fellow citizens to fork out 99 euros a piece to collectively buy the rights to the island for 99 years. The proclaimed goal was to "turn the island into a public park in which children can play and friends can have grill parties". After the decisive Internet auction, the responsible authorities did in fact decline the highest lease offer from a real estate speculator – a half million euros – as insufficient. Thus, for the time being, the island remains in the hands of the state, and who knows, maybe it really will be opened to the public soon.

A half mask is a must for Carnival

VIVALDI

He is considered *the* Italian Baroque composer and left no less than 49 operas and 477 concerti for posterity. The "Four Seasons" are mainly responsible for Vivaldi's fame throughout the world and his presence on concert programmes. However, the "Maestro di Capella", who was born in Venice in 1678, is just as important as a reformer of instrumental music, and he was the first to create the classical three-movement solo concert that is still practised today. Even more than Claudio Monteverdi, who revolutionised sacred music while he was conductor at San Marco two generations previously, Vivaldi represents the musical character of the lagoon city.

SIGHTSEEING

🏙 **WHERE TO START?**
Head for the **Piazza San Marco (126 C3)** (*⌂ J–K 7–8*) first of all – preferably on board one of the Line 1 or 2 *vaporetti* that travel along the Canal Grande from the railway station, coach and car parks on Piazzale Roma. The 4.1/4.2 and 5.1/5.2 lines are also a good way to become acquainted with Venice as they travel around the entire old town. The best bird's eye panoramas are from the viewing galleries in the Campanile of San Marco or San Giorgio Maggiore.

It has been done millions of times before: the first thing to do is to take a trip along Venice's magnificent main "boulevard", the Canal Grande.

Take a Line 1 *vaporetto* – one of those swimming trams that chug along leisurely from one stop to the next – from the railway station or from the car park on Piazzale Roma, and let the 2.5 km (1.5 miles) row of palace and church façades drift past you. And then, what many consider the real Venice experience begins: hour-long, aimless wandering through this unique maze of stone that has developed over more than a thousand years.

The *centro storico*, the old centre of Venice, consists of six districts. At first glance, you might think that their labyrinths of streets all look the same. But each one of the six *sestrieri* has its own, absolutely individual

A maze of stone as one complete work of art: magnificent palazzi, world-famous bridges and museums and atmospheric squares

flair, although one thing applies to them all: it is not always possible to plan your route exactly. There is no reason why you shouldn't let chance guide you for a couple of hours. The only way to get to know the hidden, tranquil sides of what is really Venice with its countless small attractions is by making – sometimes involuntary – detours and roundabout paths that will open up views of its cul-de-sacs and back courtyards. And, if you should get the feeling that you are well and truly lost, you are sure to come across a yellow sign pointing to "Rialto", "San Marco" or the "Ferrovia" (railway station) on one of the next corners.

Even if one omits its churches overflowing with art treasures, Venice has several dozen museums – ranging from world-famous temples of art such as the accademia, the Doge's Palace or the Collezione Peggy Guggenheim, to comparatively small collections of Murano glass, lace, icons and Judaica that are well-worth seeing.

La Serenissima has mainly its former power to thank for this abundance. The

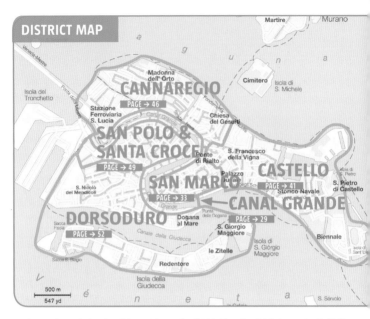

DISTRICT MAP

Martire
Murano

Venezia-Mestre

Isola del
Tronchetto

Ponte della Libertà

Madonna
dell' Orto

CANNAREGIO
PAGE → 46

Cimitero   Isola di
S. Michele

Stazione
Ferroviaria
S. Lucia

Chiesa
del Gesuiti

Canal Grande

SAN POLO &
SANTA CROCE
PAGE → 49

Ponte
di Rialto

S. Francesco
della Vigna

S. Nicolò
dei Mendicoli

SAN MARCO
PAGE → 33

Palazzo
Ducale

CASTELLO
PAGE → 41

Isola di
S. Pietro

S. Pietro
di Castello

Storico Navale

CANAL GRANDE
PAGE → 29

DORSODURO
PAGE → 52

Dogana
al Mare

Punta
della Dogana

Canale della Giudecca

S. Giorgio
Maggiore

Isola di
S. Giorgio
Maggiore

Biennale

Sacca
Fisola

Sacca S. Biagio

le Zitelle

Redentore

Isola della
Giudecca

S. Servolo

500 m
547 yd

The map shows the location of the most interesting districts. There is a detailed map of each district on which each of the sights described is numbered.

doges themselves, with their desire for prestige and their mania for collecting, amassed paintings and other valuable objects from all parts of their maritime realm and employed the best architects, painters and craftsmen at home in the city on the lagoon. With their sense of style and generosity, the nobility and rich merchant families also played a major role in assembling the wealth of unique treasures that we can feast our eyes on today.

The *scuole* are something typically Venetian. These are fraternities whose members perform charity work in the name of their chosen patron saint to benefit less privileged sections of the community. Some of the most impressive assembly houses are of inestimable value and are now open to the public as museums: the most famous is the Scuola Grande di San Rocco. The fact that the opening times and the days they are closed vary greatly and change frequently is rather impractical. And the conditions for reduced admission also vary a lot. In any case, it is always a good idea to ask if you can enter and have your passport or other means of identification with you.

Entrance fees for museums start at 5 euros (Museo Storico Navale) and go up to 9 or 10 euros (Accademia and Scuola Grande di San Rocco respectively). The *San Marco Museum Plus* pass costs 17 euros, is valid for three months, and makes it possible to visit the four museums on Piazza San Marco, as well as another of the city's collections. The *Museum Pass* for 24 euros includes all of the city's museums except the clock tower and the Palazzo Fortuny. EU citizens under the age of 18 have free entrance to the three state museums – Accademia, Galleria Franchetti and Museo d'Arte Orientale –, 18–25-year-olds are granted a reduction.

The Tourism Association's website *www.turismovenezia.it* gives the best overview on the internet (also in English and easy to navigate). All city museums are presented under *www.visitmuve.it* (also in English).

Fifteen of the most important churches in art history have joined forces to form the *Associazione Chiese di Venezia/Chorus (tel. 04 12 75 04 62 | www.chorusvenezia.org)*. The Chorus Pass, a joint ticket for 12 euros (students under 29 8 euros, families 24 euros) makes it possible to visit these houses of worship and is valid for an unlimited period. Individual entrance to the important churches costs around 3 euros.

CANAL GRANDE

Most visitors to Venice gain their initial and lasting impressions of the beauty and uniqueness of this city on board a *vaporetto* on the Canal Grande.

Travelling along this winding waterway between the Dogana del Mar, the old customs house crowned with a golden globe, and the railway station or car park on Piazzale Roma (journey time from 15 to 40 minutes) is like moving past a guard of honour made up of magnificent palaces and churches. As an exception, the most important architectural monuments along the route are listed here in their topographic order from north-west to south-east instead of alphabetically in order to make orientation less complicated.

MARCO POLO HIGHLIGHTS

★ **Museo del Settecento Veneziano**
The Ca' Rezzonico will give you an idea of the magnificent lifestyle led by the aristocracy in the 18th century → p. 32

★ **Basilica di San Marco**
Gold and silver splendour in St Mark's Cathedral → p. 33

★ **Galleria dell'Accademia**
500 years of Venetian painting, with Titian's works as highlights → p. 54

★ **Campanile di San Marco**
The best way to get an overview → p. 36

★ **Piazza San Marco**
The heart of Venice – "the most beautiful salon on earth" with elegant shops and cafés → p. 40

★ **Santi Giovanni e Paolo**
The church is the final resting place of more than two dozen doges → p. 44

★ **Frari**
Majestic basilica with Titian's altar painting and his grave → p. 49

★ **Ponte di Rialto**
The symbol of a former economic power → p. 51

★ **Palazzo Ducale**
Where the heart of the Serenissima beat for 1,000 years → p. 39

★ **Murano**
Delicate glass in the workshops and museum → p. 58

PONTE DELLA COSTITUZIONE
(120 B6) (*C–D5*)

There is a great deal of dispute about its functionality which even resulted in a legal dispute between its designer and the city. With its glass balustrade and herringbone structure, however, it is nonetheless a first-rate aesthetic triumph. This 94-metre-long pedestrian bridge designed by the Spanish master architect Santiago Calatrava has arched elegantly over the Canal Grande between Piazzale Roma and the railway station since 2008. *Stop: Piazzale Roma, Ferrovia*

FONDACO DEI TURCHI
(121 F5) (*G4*)

The complex of buildings opposite the San Marcuola *vaporetto* stop was erected in the 13th century. 400 years later, Turkish merchants lived and carried out their business here leading to the name that is commonly used today. A rather insane total redevelopment in the 19th century robbed it of its Venetian-Byzantine character. Only the characteristic towers on the sides and the wide columned hall between have been preserved. Today, the prominent building is the site of the Museum of Natural History *(Museo di Storia Naturale | June–Oct Tue–Sun 10am–6pm, Nov–May Tue–Fri 9am–5pm, Sat/Sun 10am–6pm | msn.visitmuve.it)* – great for families! The highlights include the aquarium and a dinosaur hall with a complete skeleton found in the South Sahara. *Stop: San Stae*

PALAZZO VENDRAMIN-CALERGI
(121 F4) (*G4*)

This imposing Renaissance palace built by Mauro Codussi and the Lombardo brothers around 1500 is firmly located in history as the place where Richard Wagner lived for a period before he died there on 13 February 1883. A commemorative plaque recalls that memorable day. Today, this is a gamblers' mecca; the city's *Casino (www.casinovenezia.it)* with its night club have found their home behind the windows with their round arches. *Stop: San Marcuola*

SAN STAE
(121 F5) (*G4*)

The main attraction of this 17th-century church is the beautiful Palladian-style façade added by the Swiss architect Domenico Rossi in 1709. There are several remarkable paintings from the early 18th century, including works by Giambattista Tiepolo, Giovanni Battista Piazzetta and Sebastiano Ricci, in the interior. *Campo San Stae 3013 | Mon–Sat 2pm–5pm | stop: San Stae*

CA' PESARO
(122 A5) (*H4*)

Even those who are not especially interested in the collections of oriental and modern art that are housed here should take a closer look at this massive Baroque complex with its marble façade that dominates the southern side of the Canal Grande, just two small canals away from the San Stae *vaporetto* stop. It is Baldassare Longhena's masterpiece and its construction took almost 60 years to complete. The interior is dominated by the forecourt and enormous vestibule. The splendid collection in the *Galleria d'Arte Moderna* in the Ca' Pesaro includes works by Max Klinger, Gustav Klimt, Wassily Kandinsky, Max Klee, Auguste Rodin, Marc Chagall and Giorgio De Chirico. Admirers of art from the far-east will find what they are looking for in the INSIDER TIP *Museo d'Arte Orientale* on the top floor with its collection of armour, textiles and artworks from China, Japan and Indonesia, as well as an important exhibition of Japanese

The elegant curves of Calatrava's Ponte della Costituzione crossing over the Canal Grande

paintings from the Edo period from the early 17th to mid-19th centuries. *Tue–Sun 10am–6pm, winter 10am–5pm | capesaro.visitmuve.it | stop: San Stae*

CA' D'ORO/GALLERIA GIORGIO FRANCHETTI
(122 A–B5) (𝄐 H4–5)

Nowhere else along the Canal Grande can you find a façade that is more delicate and precious than this one. The "Golden House" is the masterwork of the Venetian late-Gothic period at the transition to the Renaissance. Its painstakingly restored exterior, which was originally decorated with gold leaf and coloured marble, looks like Burano lace carved out of stone. INSIDER TIP *Baron Franchetti's art collection* is exhibited inside. It includes several masterpieces such as Andrea Mantegna's *St Sebastian*, Titian's *Venus*, Vittore Carpaccio's *Annunciation* and *Death of the Blessed Virgin*, as well as paintings by Giovanni Bellini, Giorgione, Anthony van Dyck and many other artists. There is also an admirable collection of Flemish tapestries and Gothic and Renaissance furniture. *Tue–Sun 8:15am–7:15pm, Mon 8:15am–2pm | www.cadoro.org | stop: Ca' d'Oro*

PESCHERIA
(122 B5) (𝄐 H5)

The neo-Gothic building with its arcades was only constructed in 1907. However, a fish market has been held on this location since the 14th century and the neighbouring fruit and vegetable market ever since 1100. *Stop: Rialto or Ca' d'Oro and cross with the traghetto (gondola ferry)*

FONDACO DEI TEDESCHI
(122 B–C6) (𝄐 J6)

This was once the seat of the German merchants, the most powerful colony of businessmen in the city, and the main trading and shipping centre for goods from the Orient on their way across the sea towards the Alps. The wares used to be weighed, packed and stored on the ground floor. The upper stories contained the dining rooms and 60 rooms, most of which were rented for lengthy periods by the major trading companies. The future function of this building, enclosed in scaffolding until at least 2017, which has been sold to the Benetton corporation is heavily disputed and still entirely uncertain. *Stop: Rialto*

PALAZZO GRASSI
(125 E3) *(Ⓜ F8)*

Today, this striking neo-Classicist palace designed by Giorgio Massari presents temporary exhibitions from the extensive collection of contemporary art of its present owner, the French entrepreneur François Pinault. *Wed–Mon 10am–7pm | joint ticket with Punta della Dogana | www.palazzograssi.it | stop: San Samuele*

CA' REZZONICO/MUSEO DEL
SETTECENTO VENEZIANO ★
(125 D–E4) *(Ⓜ F8)*

Even by Venetian standards, the massive palace built by Baldassare Loghena and Giorgio Massari is a special jewel of Renaissance architecture. For part of the 18th century, it was owned by Carlo Rezzonico who later wrote history as Pope Clemens XIII. Today, the building is home to the *Museo del Settecento Veneziano* and impressively documents the opulent lifestyle of the aristocracy in the late period of the Republic. The "Museum of the 18th

Century" is spread over the three floors of the *palazzo*. Meticulously renovated, the priceless furniture and decorations, paintings and ceiling paintings on display provide an authentic impression of how the wealthy noble families lived during that high point in Venice's history. The carved furnishings, ceiling frescos and cabinet paintings with scenes of everyday life in Venice by Pietro Longhi are particularly outstanding. *Entrance: Fondamenta Rezzonico | Wed–Mon 10am–6pm, winter 10am–5pm | carezzonico.visitmuve.it | stop: Ca' Rezzonico*

SANTA MARIA DELLA SALUTE
(126 A–B5) *(Ⓜ H9)*

This epitome of a Venetian Baroque church rises up in all its glory over the south-eastern end of the Canal Grande – a fantastic building, cloaked in white marble, designed by Baldassare Longhena on an octagonal layout. The church was erected in gratitude for an end to a plague epidemic and is crowned by a mighty dome that can be seen shining from far away. The vestry is decorated with altar paintings by Titian, Tintoretto and other masters. *Daily 9am–noon and 3–5:30pm | stop: Salute*

RELAX & ENJOY

If you need a break from the cramped old town, take a trip across to the Lido. The narrow 12-km-long (7.5 miles) island of sand that protects Venice and its lagoon from the open sea developed into a fashionable seaside resort towards the end of the 19th century, as those who have seen Luchino Visconti's film version of Thomas Mann's novella *Death in Venice* know. Today, things are much more

down to earth here – except when film stars hold court in the Palazzo del Cinema during the International Film Festival. But the Lido has not lost any of its quality as a perfect place for sports enthusiasts and those just looking for the *dolce far niente*; with its flat, endless Adriatic beach that invites one to swim or go for a stroll, its countless pizzerias and ice cream parlours, it has something for everybody.

PUNTA DELLA DOGANA
(126 B5) (*ⵣ J9*)

The billionaire and patron of the arts François Pinault displays a representative

Here, what is probably the most beautiful square on earth, the Piazza San Marco, invites you to relax and take a stroll. No matter how short you sightseeing tour,

The main altar of Santa Maria della Salute with a Byzantine icon of the Virgin Mary

overview of his unique collection here — including masterpieces by stars such as Jeff Koons, Richard Serra and Damien Hirst. The building that was erected in the late 17th century as the former customs house at the easternmost tip of Dorsoduro is crowned with two Atlantes and a gilded globe of the world. *Wed–Mon 10am–7pm | joint ticket with Palazzo Grassi | www.palazzograssi.it | stop: Salute*

SAN MARCO

The oldest, innermost district in the *centro storico*, that was once the heart of the Maritime Republic, is still Venice's geographical and historical core.

the Doge's Palace, St Mark's Basilica, the City Museum and the view from the Campanile are absolute musts. This urban jewel, with the sounds of salon music played by the orchestras in the cafés drifting by, is surrounded by a network of narrow streets flanked by wonderful palaces and churches that open up onto magnificent squares.

■■ BASILICA DI SAN MARCO ★ ●
(126–127 C–D3) (*ⵣ K7*)

The core of this magnificent church, with its five domes and ornately decorated arches and windows, is almost 1000 years old but its over-powering effect on all the senses is the result of numerous extensions and alterations to the architectural fabric. The structure built in the

The omnipresent Lion of St Mark is even on guard above the entrance to St Mark's Basilica

form of a Greek cross in the 11th century, in which the relics that moulded Venice's identity – the bones of Saint Mark, stolen from Alexandria in Egypt – were once preserved, still forms its heart.

Whole libraries have been filled with praise for this unique artistic shrine. Here, we can only deal with the main attractions: the incomparable stone mosaics that are, unfortunately, mostly covered by carpets; the sumptuously decorated, three-door iconostasis in the choir section (entrance with an extra ticket, to the right through the Capella di San Clemente), the high altar with the sarcophagus of Saint Mark, Sansovino's vestry door as well as his bronze figures, and the most precious treasure – the P*ala d'Oro* – a gold and enamel reredos with hundreds of precious stones created between the 10th and 14th centuries. And,

of course, the magnificent *mosaics*: they illustrate episodes from the Old and New Testaments and cover an area of more than 43,000 ft². If you want to make a close inspection of them you should climb up to the gallery from the inner main portal.

The *Tesoro*, the treasury, stores the most valuable collection of Byzantine silver and gold in the world (here, as with the Pala d'Oro, you also have to pay a small extra admission fee). Most of it came from Constantinople after the Venetians plundered it in 1204. Although much of it was seized by Napoleon and melted down, the *Tesoro* still has an impressive collection of liturgical objects, reliquaries and carvings. The *Museo Marciano* that has been established on the gallery above the vestibule is also well worth visiting. Along with priceless liturgical objects, it houses the Quadriga – four world-famous bronze horses that were probably cast in Ancient Rome.

Last but not least, there are the dazzling mosaics that were applied to the walls, arches and domes of the basilica over 800 years and which will certainly turn the visitor's head in more ways than one. They show scenes from the Old Testament (in the vestibule) and New (in the three-nave interior). Highlights include the depiction of the Holy Ghost as a dove with the Twelve Apostles in the dome closest to the main entrance, the Arch of the Passion with motifs from pre-Easter events, the Ascension Dome where the Saviour floats in a circle of stars supported by angels, and Christ as

SIGHTSEEING IN SAN MARCO

1 Basilica di San Marco	**6** Museo Archeologico Nazionale
2 Biblioteca Nazionale Marciana	**7** Museo Correr
3 Campanile di San Marco	**8** Palazzo Contarini del Bovolo
4 Giardini ex Reali	**9** Palazzo Ducale
5 Goldoni Memorial	**10** Palazzo Fortuny

11 Piazza San Marco
12 Piazzetta
13 Ponte dei Sospiri
14 Torre dell'Orologio

the blessing Pantocrator in the choir dome.

Please note that it is forbidden to take luggage into the church; it can be stored in the *Ateneo San Basso (Calle San Basso 315a | daily 9:30am–5:30pm). Basilica Mon–Sat 9:45am–5pm, Sun 2–5pm, winter until 4pm; galleries daily 9:45am–4:45pm; Pala d'Oro and Tesoro Mon–Fri 9:45am–5pm, winter until 4pm), Sat/Sun 2–5pm, winter until 4pm | www.basili casanmarco.it | stop: San Marco*

▨2 BIBLIOTECA NAZIONALE MARCIANA (126 C3) (*⑳ K8*)

Jacopo Sansovino was the Florentine architect who designed this monumen-tal Renaissance construction. The main hall of what Palladio described as "possibly the most precious, richly-decorated building to be constructed since the days of the Ancient Greeks and Romans" is adorned with paintings by Veronese and Tintoretto, with the ceiling of the anteroom bearing a work by Titian. Among the most important of the approximately 900,000 volumes and 13,000 manuscripts are Marco Polo's last will and testament and the famous map of the world drawn by the monk Fra Mauro who once lived on Venice's cemetery island. *Entrance at the Museo Correr | daily 10am–7pm, in winter 10am–5pm | joint ticket with Palazzo Ducale, Museo Correr and Museo Archeologico | www. marciana.veneziana.sbn.it | stop: Vallaresso*

▨3 CAMPANILE DI SAN MARCO ★ ⋇ (126 C3) (*⑳ K8*)

A ride in the lift up to the top of the bell tower to see the ocean of tiled roofs and gables interspersed with dozens of towers is one of the essential things to do at the start of any visit to the city. The panorama not only provides you with a first, extremely helpful orientation aid but also a feeling for the unique location and structure of the city on the lagoon. The symbol of the city was originally erected in the 10th century and considerably increased in height in the 12th. The almost 100-metre-high (330 ft) tower collapsed in 1902 but was reconstructed using the original material as much as possible. While queuing to buy tickets, you will have the opportunity to admire the Loggetta, built by Jacopo Sansovino around 1540. Venice's nobility used to like to gather for a chat under its arcades that form an architectural counterpart to the Scala dei Giganti ("Giants' Staircase") in the Doge's Palace opposite. *Easter–June and Oct daily 9am–*

7pm, July–Sept 9am–9pm, Nov–Easter 9:30am–3:45pm | stop: San Marco

4 GIARDINI EX REALI
(126 C3–4) *(∅ J–K8)*

The only oasis of green in the stony heart of the city – and a very small one at that. Not a bad place to sit down on a shady bench to get your breath back. *Stop: San Marco*

5 GOLDONI MEMORIAL
(126 B–C1) *(∅ J6)*

Even cast in bronze, Carlo Goldoni, Venice's great comedy playwright, seems to be smiling to himself. This is not surprising seeing that the *Campo San Bartolomeo* where it is located is especially popular with the Venetians as a place to come and gossip or share a drink until late at night. The charming statue was created in 1883 by the Venetian Antonio dal Zotto. *Stop: Rialto*

6 MUSEO ARCHEOLOGICO NAZIONALE
(126 C3) *(∅ K8)*

The museum has a valuable collection of Greek and Roman sculptures that certainly influenced many Venetian painters and sculptors in their work. In addition, the museum houses a great number of antique bronzes, ceramics, jewellery and coins as well as an archaeological collection with finds from ancient Egypt, Babylonia and Assyria. *Entrance through Museo Correr | daily 10am–7pm, Nov–March until 5pm | joint ticket with Biblioteca Marciana and Palazzo Ducale | www.polomuseale.venezia.beniculturali. it | stop: San Marco*

7 MUSEO CORRER
(126 B–C3) *(∅ J8)*

This city museum with its incredibly rich collections is located in the Napoleon Wing and Procuratie Nuove, behind the south-west façade of the Piazza San Marco, invites you to take a journey to the roots of Venetian (art) history. The neo-Classicist rooms on the first floor display some early works by the renowned sculptor Antonio Canova and a comprehensive overview of the major

Eye-catcher: the Campanile di San Marco

historical themes of the city on the lagoon ranging from trade and seafaring or politics, administration and war history to the arts, trade and festivities. Official robes and magnificent vestments worn by dignitaries are on display along with coins and the marble Lions of Saint

Mark, old maritime and land maps as well as the first detailed plan of the city created by Jacopo de' Barbari around 1500. One additional focus of attention is the documentation of Venetian history from the end of the Republic in 1797 to the unification of the city with the Kingdom of Italy in the 1860s. After ten years of restoration work, the re-opened INSIDER TIP imperial chambers, in which the Empress Sisi, the wife of the Hapsburg Emperor Franz Joseph, resided for a total of eight months during two trips to the city, are a new attraction at the museum.

A large section of the second floor is reserved for the picture gallery: precious paintings and sculptures from the Veneto-Byzantine and early-Gothic periods, into the cinquecento, the golden 16th century. The highlights in the more than 20 halls include works by Jacopo Bellini and his family, their contemporaries as well as Lorenzo Lotto who was active one generation later and the snow-white marble statues created by Antonio Canova. The most famous exhibit in the museum by far, however, is Vittorio Carpaccio's picture of two "Venetian Ladies" painted around 1510 that supposedly shows two smug courtesans with their dogs and birds. *Summer daily 10am–7pm, winter 10am–5pm | joint ticket with Palazzo Ducale, Biblioteca Marciana and Museo Archeologico | correr.visitmuve.it | stop: Vallaresso*

8 PALAZZO CONTARINI DEL BOVOLO
(126 B2–3) *(H7)*

If you follow a small yellow sign on the south side of Campo Marin and go around two or three corners, you will find yourself in front of this charming example of playful Renaissance architecture. The "Snail

The power and splendour of the city republic unfolds before your eyes in the Doge's Palace

Shell" (in Venetian: *bovolo*), a spiral stair-case with elegant arcades erected around the year 1500, winds its way upwards in a brick cylindrical construction on the façade of the noble Contarini family's Gothic palace. *April–Oct daily 10am–6pm, Nov–March 10am–4pm (at the time of going to press, the palazzo was closed due to restoration) | www.scalabovolo.org | stop: Rialto, Sant'Angelo*

9 PALAZZO DUCALE ★ ●
(127 D3) (*U K8*)

The most palatial of all palaces; a centre of political and legislative power, the greatest symbol of Venetian civilisation and an eye-catcher on all *vedute* of the city. Over the past 1,000 years, 120 doges guided the destiny of the Sea Republic from within its walls. In the Gothic form we see it today, most of the complex, which consists of three wings

between 70 and 100 metres (230–330 ft) in length, was constructed in the 14th and early 15th centuries.

The colossal marble façade, whose lower section is interspersed with countless delicate columns and arches, deserves our greatest admiration. Take a closer look at the wonderful sculptures of "Adam and Eve" and "Drunken Noah" on the corners of the south wing, as well as the delightful scenes on each one of the capitals of the dozens of columns! A tour of the interior of the Doge's Palace is completely overwhelming. It begins at the high-Gothic main portal, the *Porta della Carta*, opposite the Loggetta and Campanile. You pass through it to enter the inner court that is dominated by a two-storey triumphal arch, the *Arco Foscari*, and the *Scala dei Giganti* watched over by two statues, one of Neptune and one of Mars, created by Jacopo Sansavino.

The greatest Italian painters of the 16th century were involved in decorating the rooms; the most important were Tintoretto, Titian and Paolo Veronese. Most of the gigantic pictures they painted show scenes from the history of the city, from the myths surrounding its foundation to great military victories. However, the greatest impression will probably be made by the *Sala del Maggior Consiglio*, a hall measuring 54 × 25 m (177 × 82 ft) where as many as 1,800 members of the Grand Council met to elect high state officials and the members of the Signoria. Your eyes will be drawn towards Tintoretto's painting of Paradise on the end wall; at 7 × 22 m (23 × 72 ft) it is the largest painting on canvas in the world. The tour ends with a walk over the Bridge of Sighs to the New Prison.

The tours on "secret paths", *Itinerari Segreti*, which are held every day in Italian, French and English, are very special.

Tickets can be bought at the information desk at the palace entrance or online at least 48 hours in advance (visit to the palace is included in the ticket price). You will be able to visit the false ceiling of the Hall of the Great Council, the offices of the Grand Chancellor, the secret archives and the notorious "lead chambers" *(piombi)* where Giacomo Casanova was once incarcerated. *Summer daily 8:30am–7pm, winter 8:30am–5:30pm | joint ticket with Biblioteca Marciana, Museo Correr and Museo Archeologico | palazzoducale.visit muve.it | stop: San Zaccaria*

10 PALAZZO FORTUNY
   (126 A2) (∅ H7)

The Spanish-born painter Mariano Fortuny lived for more than 40 years in this Gothic *palazzo* that is so full of atmosphere. The highly-gifted artist worked as a painter, sculptor, stage designer, lighting technician, decorator and also designed magnificent silk fabrics and hand-painted lamps. The building has been totally renovated and now documents all of the facets of the work and collecting activities of this astounding personality. There are interesting temporary exhibitions on the ground floor. *Calle Pesaro 3958 | Wed–Mon 10am–6pm | fortuny.visitmuve.it | stop: Sant'Angelo*

11 PIAZZA SAN MARCO ★
   (126 C3) (∅ J–K 7–8)

Napoleon's exclamation that this is "the most beautiful salon on earth" is still valid more than two hundred years later. The 175 m/574 ft long, slightly trapezoid-shaped St Mark's Square is really unique and conjures up a different atmosphere depending on the time of day and season. It has been the site of countless religious processions and a great number of very earthly festivities. The Piazza has remained a stage for the vanity of both

The Museo Fortuny shows all facets of work by this talented Spanish all-rounder

locals and tourists alike to this very day. And, during those rare hours on foggy winter days or late at night when the usual masses have deserted it and it finally comes to rest, isolated dreamers will find it a magical setting. The buildings around this square that was first laid out more than 800 years ago are described separately in this chapter. Here, we can only recommend that you do what generations of travellers before you have done, stroll through the arcades with their luxury shops and across the square and inhale the atmosphere of the incessant flow of people and the unique setting. *Stop: San Marco*

12 PIAZZETTA
(126–127 C–D3) *(ⵍ K8)*

The elongated area between the Campanile and Canale di San Marco, flanked on the east by the Doge's Palace and on the west by the Biblioteca Marciana, has fulfilled many functions over the centuries. For a period, gambling took place here in the open air, market stalls were set up, as were latrines, and public executions also took place here. Now it is a meeting place for people on a stroll through the city and souvenir sellers. All of these activities are watched over by Venice's first patron saint Theodor – accompanied by his crocodile – and a winged Lion of Saint Mark on top of two massive columns. *Stop: San Marco*

13 PONTE DEI SOSPIRI
(127 D3) *(ⵍ K8)*

You will almost imagine that you can still hear the sighs of the prisoners who once made their way, protected from any curious onlookers, over this draughty corridor from the courtroom in the Doge's Palace to the New Prison *(Palazzo delle Priogioni)*. But, only almost, because the incessant chatter of the hordes of tourists and the

clicking of the cameras shooting away at the Bridge of Sighs from the *Ponte della Paglia* on the quay drown out everything. *Stop: San Zaccaria*

14 TORRE DELL'OROLOGIO (CLOCK TOWER) ⛴
(126 C3) *(ⵍ K7)*

With its blue and white façade, crowned with a Lion of Saint Mark and the large dial, the clock tower designed by Mauro Codussi sometime around 1500 marks the spot where the Mercerie enters the Piazza di San Marco. From the roof terrace, two bronze giants deafeningly strike the hour. It is only possible to enter the tower on a guided tour *(information and reservations tel. 0 41 42 73 08 92)* | *Piazza San Marco* | *stop: San Marco*

CASTELLO

The largest of Venice's *sestrieri* offers a great variety of different moods: immediately behind the Doge's Palace and along the Riva Degli Schiavoni, there is the hustle and bustle of tourist life and a row of luxury hotels next to each other, but a little further east, around Via Garibaldi and in the winding streets where the shipyard workers used to live, it is much more intimate.

Small workshops, stores, narrow streets with clotheslines overhead and children playing: this is where Venice shows its friendly, everyday – occasionally a little impoverished – side. But, there are also many magnificent artistic treasures waiting to be discovered here too – churches such as San Zaccaria and Santi Giovanni e Paolo with the doges' graves, or the *scuole* of the Dalmatians and Greeks. The largest green area in the city, the Giardini Pubblici, will give you a chance to catch a breath of fresh air. This is where the

A pack of lions guard the gate at the entrance to the Arsenale

18th century and consequently heavily guarded. Today, ferries and freighters are repaired in the 320,000 m² (80 acres) area with its magnificent entrance (*Ingresso di Terra*) flanked by four lions. This is also the site of several high-tech companies, workshops and offices. Today, the Italian military forces still preside over a small section. Tourists have two possibilities to see inside Europe's first production-line factory: either as a visitor to the Biennale that temporarily uses some of the halls for exhibitions, or by taking part in one of the INSIDER TIP special guided tours (*bookings four weeks in advance, at least 6 persons | www.vogliadarte.it*). *Stop: Arsenale*

2 CAMPO DI SANTA MARIA FORMOSA
(127 D1) (*K–L6*)

Theatre performances, festivals and bull-fights used to be held here on one of the largest and most beautiful squares in Venice. These spectacles, however, are all things of the past. But, this is still a great place to have an ice cream or cup of coffee and watch everyday life go by around the rather isolated Santa Maria Formosa Church – by Venetian standards. *Stop: San Zaccaria*

3 COLLEONI MONUMENT
(123 D6) (*L5*)

The mercenary leader Bartolomeo Colleoni was really a sly one: when he died in 1475, he left his immense fortune to the Republic – on the condition that a gigantic statue of him be set up in front of San Marco. Of course, he meant St Mark's Cathedral. But the doges showed that they were even craftier and immortalised the meritorious man – who came from Bergamo and was, therefore, a "foreigner" – not in front of the basilica, but the Scuola of the same name. But that doesn't change anything:

Biennale, a show of what is happening in the world of contemporary art, is held every two years. The shipyard, the Arsenale, is a deserted alien element that, even today, is absolutely off-limits to the unauthorised.

1 ARSENALE
(128–129 B–D 1–3) (*N–P 6–8*)

This shipyard, where Venice built all the ships for its gigantic navy and merchant fleet, and where weapons and gunpowder were also stored, was the centre of the largest sea power in the Eastern Mediterranean from the 14th to the late

the bronze equestrian statue cast by the Florentine sculptor Andrea Verrocchio is one of the most magnificent Renaissance monuments in all of Italy. *Campo Santi Giovanni e Paolo | stop: Ospedale*

4 GIARDINI PUBBLICI
(129 D5–6) (*ω P–Q 10–11*)

Lawns and avenues of trees are rare in Venice. But, if you feel like you really need to take a stroll around a garden, then this is for you. *Stop: Giardini*

5 INSIDER TIP MUSEO QUERINI STAMPALIA
(127 D2) (*ω L7*)

This impressive collection of paintings is the highlight of any tour of this splendid patrician's house. It includes works by Giovanni Bellini, Palma il Vecchio and Giambattista Tiepolo, as well as the delightful genre scenes of everyday life in Venice by Pietro Longhi and Gabriele Bella. The tour through a total of 20 rooms is especially fascinating because it will give you an idea of the magnificent surroundings the wealthy nobility of the 18th century, like Count Querini Stampilia, lived in. They would socialise beneath opulent ceiling frescos, Rococo stucco and chandeliers made of Murano glass, between magnificent mirrors, lacquer furniture and the walls of the library with 200,000 books on its shelves. *Tue–Sun 10am–6pm | www.querinistampalia.it | stop: San Zaccaria*

6 MUSEO STORICO NAVALE ●
(128 B4) (*ω N–O8*)

The Museum of Naval History is fittingly housed in an old warehouse right next to the Arsenal and covers the history of the maritime republic from the perspective of shipping. There are many models of battle and passenger ships, canons from five centuries, explanations of how gondolas and fortresses are built, as well as fishing nets, nautical charts, navigational equipment and pious votive pictures testifying to miraculous rescues at sea. The highlight is definitely the "Bucintoro", the state galley from which the doge performed the annual "Marriage of the Sea" ritual. On weekends, an INSIDER TIP extra tour through the Ships Pavilion, a huge collection of historic vessels, is worthwhile. *Mon–Thu 8:45am–1:30pm, Fri–Sun 8:45am–5pm, ships' pavilion tour start Sat/Sun 2pm and 3:30 pm, Sun also 11am and 12:30pm | msn.visitmuve.it | stop: Arsenale*

The highlight in the Museo Storico Navale: the golden Bucintoro

■7 SAN FRANCESCO DELLA VIGNA
(128 A1) (*ⁿ N6*)

There is one main reason for visitors coming to this Franciscan church in the somewhat remote north-east corner of Castello: its façade, that is reminiscent of an ancient temple, was designed by none other than Andrea Palladio. While you are here, you should also go inside and see the Madonna by Paolo Veronese and Giovanni Bellini's *Mother of God*. *Daily 8am–12:30pm and 3–6pm | stop: Celestia*

■8 SAN GIORGIO DEI GRECI/
MUSEO DIPINTI SACRI BIZANTINI
(127 E2) (*ⁿ M7*)

The spiritual heart of what was once a very wealthy Greek colony with several thousand members was built in the 16th and renovated in the 17th century following plans drawn up by Baldassare Longhena: strikingly narrow, high, with beautifully carved choir stalls and a dazzling iconostasis. But don't worry: according to the structural engineers, the precariously sloping campanile will remain standing for quite some time...

There is a small but excellent museum next door with around 150 icons that were painted between the 13th and 17th centuries in Greece, the Veneto and on Crete. *Calle dei Greci | Church Mon–Sat 9am–12:30pm and 2:30–4:30pm, Sun 9am–1pm, museum daily 9am–5pm | www.istitutoellenico.org | stop: San Zaccaria*

■9 SANTI GIOVANNI E PAOLO ★
(123 D–E6) (*ⁿ L5*)

The importance official Venice attached to the Dominicans as the order that commissioned this house of worship can be seen by the fact that no fewer than 27 doges have found their final resting places here. The graves give an impressive lesson in how the local art of sculpture developed from the late-Gothic to the Baroque periods. It reaches its pinnacle in the grave of Alvise Mocenigo that takes up the entire space of the inner church portal. The Baroque altar opposite it, designed by Baldassare Longhena, is hardly any less massive. The overall impression of the interior of this mendicant order's

THE VOGALONGA ROWING EVENT

The city on the lagoon offers rowing fans an unforgettable spectacle that is absolutely unique worldwide: every year, on a Sunday at the end of May, Venice comes under the spell of the ★ *Vogalonga*, a 30 km (18.5 miles) rowing marathon with more than 5,000 amateur participants leaning into the oars. The more than 1,500 vessels – all classes, from canoe and gondola, to rowing and dragon boats are allowed – create a tremendously colourful picture and great fun is had by all. The route starts at the Bacino San Marco and takes the rowers all the way to Burano and back to the *centro storico* by way of Murano. The most popular places to watch the spectacle are the Riva degli Schiavoni, the main canal in Murano, Canal di Cannaregio and the Canal Grande. Around half of the participants come from abroad. Anybody with a boat and enough muscle power can take part. Information and registration: *tel. 04 15 21 05 44 | www.vogalonga.it*

SIGHTSEEING IN CASTELLO

- **1** Arsenale
- **2** Campo di Santa Maria Formosa
- **3** Colleoni monument
- **4** Giardini Pubblici
- **5** Museo Querini Stampalia
- **6** Museo Storico Navale
- **7** San Francesco della Vigna
- **8** San Giorgio dei Greci/ Museo Dipinti Sacri Bizantini
- **9** Santi Giovanni e Paolo
- **10** San Zaccaria
- **11** Scuola di San Giorgio degli Schiavoni

church is conspicuously ascetic but it is enhanced by some magnificent works of art including paintings by Giovanni Bellini, Lorenzo Lotto and Paolo Veronese. It is worth taking a closer look at the Renaissance façade of the immediately adjacent *Scuola Grande di San Marco* with its wonderful reliefs and marble intarsia; today, this is a hospital.

Mon–Sat 9am–6pm, Sun noon–6pm, please note: these times change frequently | stop: Ospedale

10 SAN ZACCARIA
(123 E3) *(∅ L7)*
The marble façade of this church only two or three minutes walk from the Doge's Palace is a real feast for the eyes

and there are several important artworks in the interior, including one of Giovanni Bellini's most important paintings, the beautiful *Sacra Conversazione* (Maria

gilded panelling. Its greatest treasure is the cycle of paintings created at the beginning of the 16th century by Vittore Carpaccio. It shows scenes from

One of the four synagogues in the ghetto is the Scuola Levantina

with Child). The campanile was part of the former church erected in the 12th century and this makes it one of the oldest bell towers in Venice. *Mon–Sat 10am–noon and 4pm–6pm, Sun 4pm–6pm, please note: these times change frequently | stop: San Zaccaria*

the life of the three patron saints of Dalmatia – George, Trifon and Hieronymus – painted with the airy elegance so typical of this artist. *Mon 2:45–6pm, Tue–Sat 9:15am–1pm and 2:45–6pm, Sun 9:15am–1pm | stop: San Zaccaria*

⑪ SCUOLA DI SAN GIORGIO DEGLI SCHIAVONI
(127 F2) (⑭ M7)

The brotherhood of the Slavonic people was founded in 1452 by wealthy Dalmatian merchants with the aim of supporting impoverished, old seamen from their homeland and providing education for their children. The small oratory is one of the few rooms in the city where the paintings are still surrounded by their original carved and

CANNAREGIO

The old centre of this district in the north-west, between the railway station and Rialto Bridge, Canal Grande and the lagoon, reveals itself as surprisingly bright and airy.

The broad canals, flooded with light, are perfect for a peaceful stroll. This is also where trendy pubs and bars frequented by many young people invite you to linger for a while until late at night. By Venetian standards, the unusually straight main route (Lista di Spagna/Rio Terà San Leonardo/Strada Nova), from the railway station towards Rialto Bridge and San Marco, with its countless shops and small markets is crowded with tourists. Here, and on the north bank of the Canal Grande, which runs parallel to it, many magnificent palaces await discovery. You should definitely visit the Ghetto in the heart of this district, not only on account of its beautiful synagogue but also for the unique history of this place, and to feel its mysterious, melancholy atmosphere.

■ CHIESA DEI GESUITI
(122 C4) *(∅ K 3–4)*

A little bit off the usual tourist track, on the north-eastern border of Cannaregio, a classic example of Venetian high-Baroque architecture rises into the sky: the main church of the Jesuit Order that was not always warmly welcomed in St Mark's Republic. The façade, with its colossal columns and elaborate sculptural decoration, creates a striking first impression. The painstakingly renovated interior, with its shades of green and white, is even more impressive. Your eyes will be drawn towards the elaborate high alter designed by Giuseppe Pozzo. The most precious decoration, however, is Titian's amazingly expressive painting of the torture of St Laurentius in the first chapel of the left-hand nave. *Campo dei Gesuiti | daily 10am–noon and 4–7pm, in winter 10am–6pm | stop: Fondamenta Nuove*

■ GHETTO
(121 E3) *(∅ F 2–3)*

Located in the centre of Cannaregio, this "district within a district" has the rather dubious honour of having served as a kind of model for all the ghettos created later throughout the world. At the beginning of the 16th century, the Senate allocated this district to be the home of the 5,000 members of the very successful and influential Jewish community. This area, whose name comes from the metal foundries – the *getti* – that were formerly located here, was conveniently surrounded by canals. Gates were added and manned by – Christian – guards, and blocks of flats were built that were rented to Jews at exorbitant rates. The names of the three sections are misleading; the "new" Ghetto Nuovo is actually 25 years older than the "old" Ghetto Vecchio. The "newest" Ghetto Nuovissimo was created when the area was extended around 1630.

The four magnificent synagogues in the Ghetto are well worth visiting: the *Scuola La Tedesca* built in 1528 by German Ashkenazi Jews, the four year younger *Scuola Canton* that is now in the Rococo style, the *Scuola Levantina* from the second half of the 17th century with its splendidly carved pulpit by Andrea Brustolon and the largest *Scuola Spagnola* that is especially impressive on account of the use of multi-coloured marble. The very informative guided tours also include a visit to the *Museo Ebraico (Sun–Fri – except on Jewish holidays – 10am–7pm, winter 10am–5:30pm | www.museoebraico.it)* where precious torah shrines, silver candelabras, documents, textiles, furniture and musical instruments bring the rich tradition of Venice's Jewish community back to life. *Tours Sun–Fri (except on Jewish holidays) in Italian and English every hour 10:30am–5:30pm (winter until 4:30pm) | meeting place at the Museum | stop: Guglie*

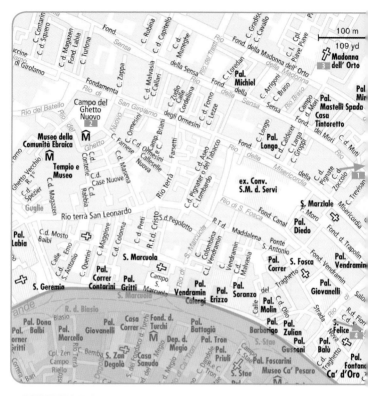

SIGHTSEEING IN CANNAREGIO

1 Chiesa dei Gesuiti
2 Ghetto
3 Madonna dell'Orto
4 Santa Maria dei Miracoli

3 MADONNA DELL'ORTO
(122 A2) (*H2*)

An artistic jewel that is unjustly neglected: the brick façade of this Gothic church in the north with its statues of the Apostles and finely carved windows is a feast for the eyes. And there are a number of INSIDER TIP top class paintings in the interior including *John the Baptist* by Cima da Conegliano and several works by Tintoretto, who is buried in the apse. *Mon–Sat 10am–5pm, Sun noon–5pm | stop: Madonna dell'Orto*

4 INSIDER TIP SANTA MARIA DEI MIRACOLI
(122 C6) (*K5*)

The charm of this church makes itself felt even more since extensive renovation work was completed at the end of the 1990s. Its façade with marble panels of varying colours and the extensive, filigree stonemason's work in the single-nave interior are inimitably exquisite. *Mon–Sat 10am–5pm | stop: Rialto*

SAN POLO & SANTA CROCE

The city started to grow from this core area west of Rialto Bridge more than 1,000 years ago.

The old trading and banking district on the Canal Grande has hardly lost any of its former bustling activity: the many shops, the fish, fruit and vegetable markets make a stroll around here a feast for the senses. The many palaces and churches, with Santa Maria Gloriosa dei Frari in first place, and the neighbouring Scuola Grande di San Rocco also make it an important hunting ground for art lovers. The best place to watch this hive of activity over a cappuccino or *ombra* – a small glass of wine – is on Campo San Polo, the second largest open space in the city, or in the area between Pescheria and Rialto where many chic shops have breathed new life into the area.

◼ CAMPO SAN POLO
(125 F1–2) *(𝄞 G6)*

With its shaded benches and open-air cafés, this gigantic open space is the perfect place to take a rest and enjoy the unique atmosphere. *Stop: San Silvestro*

◼ FRARI ★
(125 E2) *(𝄞 F6)*

Along with the Dominican church of Santi Giovanni e Paolo, the "Frari", as Santa Maria Gloriosa dei Frari is called for short, is the second largest Gothic church of the mendicant order in the city. In contrast with their self-imposed humility and the building's modest exterior, its commissioners, the Franciscans, did not hide their light under a bushel in the interior. A tour of the Frari reveals it as an artistic treasure house of the highest quality. The first thing you will notice in the enormous nave is the pyramidal tomb of Antonio Canova with Titian's grave and his *Pesaro Madonna* opposite. There are precious altarpieces by Bartolomeo Vivarini and Giovanni Bellini, as well as a statue of St John by Donatello in the choir chapels and sacristy where the composer Claudio Monteverdi is also buried.

Coloured marble in all its forms: Santa Maria dei Miracoli

However, the most fascinating eye-catcher is the painting above the high altar. Titian's floating *Assunta* (Ascension of the Virgin Mary) was a stroke of genius on the part of the artist; its incredible colouration and composition, striving dramatically upwards towards the heavens, were something completely new at the end of the Renaissance and already point towards the Baroque. *Mon–Sat 9am–6pm, Sun 1–6pm | stop: San Tomà*

▶3 PALAZZO MOCENIGO
(121 F5) (*M G4–5*)

Located directly behind Ca' Pesaro and San Stae Church, this magnificent early-17th century palace, with is priceless furniture, chandeliers, textiles and other decorative objects, gives a good idea of the luxury in which the nobility of the period liked to indulge. A study centre for the history of textiles and fashion has been established in some of its stately rooms; its library can also be visited by

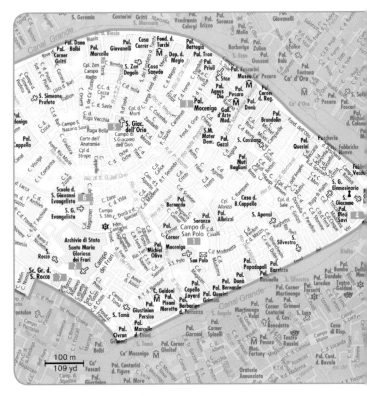

SIGHTSEEING IN SAN POLO & SANTA CROCE

Over or under it: the Rialto Bridge is a must

those who are interested. *Palace Tue–Sun 10am–5pm (winter until 4pm), Study Centre and Library Tue and Thu 8:30am–5pm, Wed and Fri 8:30am–1:30pm | stop: San Stae*

🔷 PONTE DI RIALTO ⭐
(126 B1) (*∅ J6*)

Hard-working statisticians have counted that more than 400 bridges help one cross the around 150 canals in Venice and join many of the more than 100 islands. Some are unnamed, some rather nondescript. Others play an important role for traffic or are of special artistic interest, or have become popular as meeting places – or world-famous photo motifs such as Rialto Bridge. For centuries, this site was the centre of business in the the trading metropolis of Venice. It was here that merchants unloaded their goods from far away lands and the most important banks and trading companies set up their offices.

In its present form, the bridge joining the *sestrieri* of San Marco and San Polo was constructed using stone from Istria at the end of the 16th century to replace its rotting, wooden predecessor. Until the middle of the 19th century, it was the only way for pedestrians to cross the Canal Grande. Its architect was a certain Antonio da Ponte whose – not especially elegant, but solid – design, allowing sufficient room for boats to pass beneath it, won against competitors of the ilk of Michelangelo, Palladio, Sansovino and Scamozzi. *Stop: Rialto*

🔷 INSIDER TIP ▶ SAN GIACOMO DELL'ORIO (121 E5–6) (*∅ F5*)

This church, founded in the 9th century and extended several times after that, is located on a shady, dreamy square. You will be charmed by the archaic atmosphere and strange hotchpotch of styles in the interior and should pay special attention to the paintings by Lorenzo Lotto on the main altar and by Paolo Veronese in the left transept. *Mon–Sat 10am–5pm | stop: Riva di Biasio*

6 SCUOLA GRANDE DI SAN GIOVANNI EVANGELISTA (125 D–E1) (*ⓜ F5–6*)

This Renaissance gem was founded in 1261 by one of the many flagellant orders of the period and dedicated to St John the Evangelist. The elaborately carved courtyard entrance and double flight of stairs are especially interesting. However, it is only possible to visit the interior of the *scuola* by appointment *(tel. 04 17 18 234)* or during one of the regular concerts, opera performances or art exhibitions. *Calle dell'Olio 2454 | www.scuola disangiovanni.it | stop: San Tomà*

7 SCUOLA GRANDE DI SAN ROCCO (125 D2) (*ⓜ E–F6*)

Someone not struck dumb by the treasures in this meeting house is probably not moved by any form of art at all! The walls and ceilings of this building dedicated to Saint Roch, who gave protection from the Plague, are decorated with no fewer than 56 paintings, created over a period of 18 years in the late 16th century by Jacopo Robusti, better known as Tintoretto. They show scenes from the Old and New Testaments. With its perfect proportions and magnificent coffered ceiling, the main hall on the upper floor is considered one of the most exquisite rooms in all of Italy. The adjacent hostel *(Sala dell'Albergo)* with Tintoretto's *Crucifixion* of 1565 is hardly any less impressive. The eight large-format paintings of the life of the Virgin Mary in the – rather gloomy – entrance hall on the ground floor are also well worth seeing. A few years ago, the *Scoletta di San Rocco (daily 9:30am– 6pm)* opposite the *scuola grande* opened its doors to visitors. It is quite charming but considerably more modestly decorated and is now used for interesting temporary exhibitions. On no account should you miss *San Rocco Church (daily 9:30am–5:30pm)* next door with its magnificent Tintoretto paintings. *Daily 9:30am–5:30pm | www. scuolagrandesanrocco.it | stop: San Tomà*

DORSODURO

Venice's "strong backbone", the *sestiere* in the south-west of the old town, presents itself as a charming mixture of rustic provinciality (during the day) and – thanks to the university nearby – student dynamism (in the evening) on its main square, Campo Santa Margherita, and in its side streets.

The proletarian traditions of the city can be seen and felt on its outskirts, especially on the island of Giudecca to the south and in the west near the harbour – and both areas are part of Dorsoduro. The rather run-down industries and businesses make these areas appear quite poor and, in some places, pretty dire.

● *Zattere,* the promenade along the Giudecca Canal, is the perfect place to take in some sun in winter. The view across the water to Palladio's churches is an absolute dream. Art lovers' hearts will start to beat faster further to the east, between the Accademia, the Guggenheim Gallery and Santa Maria della Salute. It is definitely worth making a detour to the monastery island of San Giorgio Maggiore, not only to admire the fantastic panoramic view from the *campanile* (read more about it in the Palladio walk in the "Discovery Tours" chapter).

1 CAMPO SANTA MARGHERITA (125 D3) (*ⓜ E7*)

The long, narrow main square of the Dorsoduro *sestiere* offers a strange mixture: on the one hand, its is probably Venice's most folksy *campo* – with a fish and vegetable market, wine bars and an everyday lifestyle similar to that in a village.

On the other, it is in the centre of an extremely lively youth and student scene that has developed in recent years with countless bars, pubs and cabaret theatres between Campo San Pantalon in the

by Cima da Congeliano (in the second wall altar) and Lorenzo Lotto's *St Nicholas* above the opposite altar can be admired behind the brick façade and threateningly skewwhiff baroque *campanile*. There are also performances of **INSIDER TIP** operas in period costumes several times a week *(www.musicain-maschera.it)*. *Stops: San Basilio, Ca' Rezzonico*

The Ponte del Pugni spans over the Rio di San Barnaba in Dorsoduro

north and Rio di San Barnaba in the south.

The Carmelite order's church of *Santa Maria del Carmine (Mon–Sat 7am–noon and 2:30–7pm)*, mostly just called Carmini, and its *Scuola Grande dei Carmine (daily 11am–5pm)*, decorated with paintings by Giambattista Tiepolo, form the south-west end of the Campo. A beautiful *Adoration of the Shepherds*

◪ COLLEZIONE PEGGY GUGGENHEIM
● (125 F5) (*ØJ G9*)

Cubism and Surrealism, Action Painting and abstract art – there is no movement in classical modern art that Peggy Guggenheim, a rich heiress and patron of the arts, did not collect in her Palazzo Venier dei Leoni. The low building has become a mecca for lovers of 20th-century art. Among the great painters and

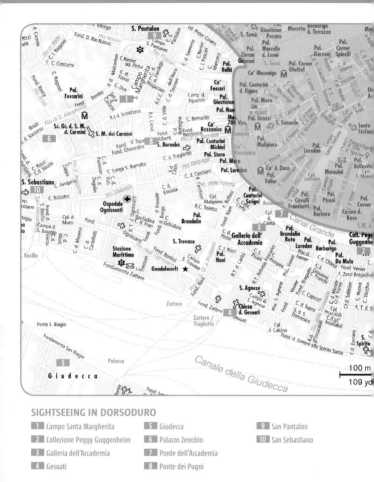

SIGHTSEEING IN DORSODURO

1 Campo Santa Margherita
2 Collezione Peggy Guggenheim
3 Galleria dell'Accademia
4 Gesuati
5 Giudecca
6 Palazzo Zenobio
7 Ponte dell'Accademia
8 Ponte dei Pugni
9 San Pantalon
10 San Sebastiano

sculptors on display here are Joan Mirò, René Magritte, Henri Matisse, Henry Moore, Piet Mondrian, Wassily Kandinsky, Georges Braque, Paul Klee, Jackson Pollock and many, many more. The most famous paintings include Picasso's *On the Beach,* Marcel Duchamp's *Sad Young Man in a Train,* Giorgio di Chirico's *The Red Tower* and *The Robing of the Bride* by Max Ernst. *Wed–*

Mon 10am–6pm | www.guggenheim-venice.it | stops: Accademia, Salute

3 GALLERIA DELL'ACCADEMIA ★ ●
   (125 E5) (*M F9*)

Bellini, Carpaccio, Giorgione, Tintoretto, Titian and Veronese, Canaletto, Guardi, Longhi, Mantegna, Lotto, Piazzetta and Tiepolo... There is hardly a single prominent representative of the more than

500-year history of Venetian painting who has not found a place in this museum on the southern bank of the Canal Grande. It is no wonder that this art gallery is considered one of the most important in the world. Don't be put off by the long queues of visitors that sometimes line up in front of the neo-Classicist façade: it is well worth being patient and waiting to see what is on display in the two dozen rooms of the spacious complex of buildings that was developed out of the former church, monastery and Scuola della Carità. If you do not want to wait too long, you can book in advance for a fixed time *(tel. 04 15 20 03 45)* at an extra charge of 1.50 euros.

The following of the more than 800 masterpieces are of particular importance in the history of art: several Madonnas painted by Giovanni Bellini, Gentile Bellini's *Miracle of the Relic of the Cross*, Vittore Carpaccio's "Legend of St Ursula" cycle, Giorgione's *The Tempest* and *Old Woman*, various Old Testament scenes and portraits of saints by Tintoretto and Paolo Veronese, as well as scenes of everyday life by Pietro Longhi, landscapes and views of cities by Canaletto and Francesco Guardi. And finally, Tiziano Vecellio, alias Titian: this giant among the masters of the Renaissance is represented with a wonderful painting of John the Baptist, his last work, *Pietà*, and *The Presentation of the Virgin Mary*, the only painting by Titian that is still in the place it was intended for. *Tue–Sun 8:15am–7:15pm, Mon 8:15am–2pm | www.galleriaacca demia.org | stop: Accademia*

Magritte, Matisse, Miró, Mondrian and Modigliani: a mecca of modern art

An island skirting the city of islands: Giudecca

connected with each other. In the Middle Ages, this was the home of the Jews *guidei* (from which the name probably stems) who had been expelled from the city. Later, rich Venetians built their summer villas here, followed, in the 19th century, by trade and industry.

Today, the main reason for visiting this area of the city, which is under the administration of the Dorsoduro *sestiere*, is to see Palladio's two churches: Redentore and Zitelle. Well-heeled guests book into the five-star Cipriani Hotel on the eastern tip. The former Molino Stuck grain mill in the west, which partially burned down in 2003, has come back to life as a luxurious Hilton Hotel. *Stops: Zitelle, Redentore, Palanca*

■ 4 GESUATI
(125 E6) (*∅ F9*)

On your stroll along the picturesque Zattere quay, it is worth taking some time to visit this sacred building designed by the great Venetian architect of the Baroque period, Giorgio Massari, to admire the beautiful ceiling frescos by Giambattista Tiepolo and altarpieces by Tintoretto, Giovanni Battista Piazzetta and Sebastiano Ricci. *Mon–Sat 10am–5pm | stop: Zattere*

■ 5 GIUDECCA ☒
(131 D4) (*∅ C–K 10–12*)

This island to the south of the old city is actually made up of eight smaller ones

■ 6 INSIDER TIP ▶ PALAZZO ZENOBIO
(124 B–C4) (*∅ D8*)

This palace, which was built in the late 17th century, was used by Armenian monks as a boarding school for more than 150 years. Now, this stately building functions as a youth hostel. It is possible to visit its greatest treasure, the sumptuously decorated ballroom, during the Biennale *(at other times, by appointment | tel. 04 15 22 87 70). Stop: San Basilio*

■ 7 PONTE DELL'ACCADEMIA
(125 E4–5) (*∅ F–G 8–9*)

When it was erected in 1932, this wooden bridge was only planned to be a temporary replacement for its predecessor that was too low for *vaporetto* traffic. But, as is often the case with interim solutions, the Venetians have become used to it and no longer want to be without it when they – and all of the visitors from far and near – admire the wonderful view down the canal towards Salute and, in the opposite direction, to Palazzo Balbi at the mouth of the Rio Foscari. *Stop: Accademia*

8 PONTE DEI PUGNI
(125 D4) (*E8*)

Four footprints have been let into the top of the "Bridge of Fists". They are there as a reminder of a custom that was upheld well into the 18th century: young Venetian men held ritual wrestling and boxing matches on the bridge and attempted to force their opponents into the water. On weekdays a sailing boat lies at anchor next to the bridge – and has been turned into a fruit and vegetable shop! *Stop: Ca' Rezzonico*

9 INSIDER TIP SAN PANTALON ●
(125 D2) (*E7*)

A little-known sensation lies waiting behind this modest – or one could say, completely blank – façade: a gigantic ceiling painting made up of 40 individual canvas elements that will really turn your head in more ways than one. Gian Antonio Fumiani was the man who worked for 24 years (!) to create this colossal Baroque work at the end of the 17th century. *Mon–Sat 10am–noon and 1–3pm | stop: San Tomà*

10 SAN SEBASTIANO
(124 B4) (*D8*)

The hearts of those who admire the cheerful, opulent paintings of Paolo Veronese will beat faster in this church. What, at first glance, appears to be a rather modest church preserves the artistic legacy of this genius. He painted all the paintings on the walls and the high altar and found his final resting place beneath the church's organ. *Mon–Sat 10am–5pm | stop: San Basilio*

THE ISLANDS

No exploration of Venice would be complete without visiting at least two or three of the islands off the coast of the *centro storico.*

The view over the lagoon alone makes the trip on the *vaporetto* an unforgettable experience. The small island of Murano is only 15 minutes away by boat and a visit to it and one of its glass-blowing workshops is a classic. On the way, you can stop off at San Michele, the cemetery island. Burano, famous for its lacework, and Torcello, with its time-honoured cathedral, lie further to the north-west. It is also worth visiting the Armenian monks on the monastery island of San Lazzaro.

BURANO ●
(131 E3) (*W–X 1–2*)

This little island is famous for its fine lacework *(merletti)* and, with its tiny, colourfully-painted houses, miniature canals and little bridges looks like a toy version of Venice. The *San Martino Church (daily 8am–noon and 3pm–7pm)* with the young Giambattista Tiepolo's *Calvary* is especially noteworthy. A visit to one of the lace-making schools or the *Museo del Merletto (in summer Tue–Sun 10am–6pm, winter 10am–5pm)* can be recommended. *Stop: Burano*

CIMITERO DI SAN MICHELE ●
(123 F1–2) (*M–N 1–3*)

Venice's cemetery island awaits its elegiac visitors halfway to Murano. Thousands of anonymous Venetians have been laid to rest under the cypresses behind the brick walls, as have some prominent visitors from abroad including the composer Igor Stravinsky, the poet Ezra Pound and the great Russian dancer Sergei Diaghilev. *Daily 7:30am–6pm (in winter until 4pm) | stop: Cimitero*

LIDO
(131 D–E4) *(∅ 0)*

From time immemorial, this 12-km-long (7.5 miles) and up to 4-km wide (2.5 miles) strip of sand has protected the city from storms and flooding. Since the 19th century, it has also served the Venetians as a place to spend their leisure time and guests from abroad as a seaside resort. In the early days of tourism, mainly the nobility, the rich and powerful of Europe, as well as privileged artists, enjoyed the *dolce far niente* on the fine sand of the Lido's beach. The splendid villas, hotels and parks are evidence of this. The bombastic ● *Grand Hotel des Bains* became famous as the scene of Thomas Mann's novella "Death in Venice" and its perfectly matched film version by Luchino Visconti. A little further west, international film stars have a rendezvous at Venice's international film festival, the Mostra del Cinema at the beginning of September in the Palazzo del Cinema, where in 2012 a new hall was opened. Many actors choose to stay in the neighbouring Hotel Excelsior, with its strangely Moorish atmosphere.

The aristocratic flair has largely vanished, but the atmosphere and infrastructure for carefree seaside holidays has remained. There are well cared-for beaches with inviting pizzerias, ice cream parlours and bars waiting for sun worshippers and keen swimmers within walking distance of the main road Viale Santa Maria Elisabetta. Night-owls will find several discos, hobby sports enthusiasts rowing and sailing clubs, a golf course nearby in Alberoni and a network of cycle tracks all over the Lido and the neighbouring Lido di Pellestrina to the south.

It is worth visiting the old San Nicolò Jewish Cemetery near the northern tip of the Lido, the INSIDER TIP ▶ *Antico Cimitero Ebraico (April–Oct by appointment | tel. 0 41 71 53 59)* and, not far away, the *Aeroporto Nicelli,* an architectural gem in the Bauhaus style that has recently been brought back to life.

Those who are interested can take the ferry from Ca' Roman, a small conservation area in the south-west, to the mainland and then travel by bus or – even better – by bike (rental at the Lido *vaporetto* stop, *www.lidoonbike.it)* to Chioggia. But, strictly speaking, this colourful, lively fishing town does not really belong to Venice and is more oriented on the mainland and sea than the lagoon. *Stops: Lido, San Nicolò*

MURANO ★
(131 D3) *(∅ P–S 1–4)*

Comprising five islands and inhabited for around 1,400 years, this community (pop. today: almost 7,000) is famous for its glass industry. A visit to one of the workshops is an absolute must as is the *Museo del Vetro (daily 10am–6pm, in winter until 5pm | stop: Museo)*. With more than 4,000 exhibits, this museum in the Palazzo Giustinian documents the 1,000-year history of glass-blowing on Murano. There are even Roman glass objects on display.

The Romanesque former *Santi Maria e Donato Cathedral (Mon–Sat 9am–noon and daily 3:30–7pm),* with its two-storey arcades in the choir section and original mosaic floor, as well as the *San Pietro Martire Church (Mon–Fri 8am–7pm, Sat 11am–7pm, Sun noon–5pm)* with one of Giovanni Bellini's major works, will be of particular interest to art lovers. *Various stops*

SAN LAZZARO DEGLI ARMENI
(131 D4) *(∅ 0)*

This island not far from the Lido was used as a isolation hospital for lepers for hundreds of years. In the 18th century, it was placed in the hands of monks of the Armenian Mekhitarist order. Their monastery *Monastero Mekhitarista*, with a small museum, picture gallery and valuable library, is the only attraction on the island – but is well-worth seeing. *Tours daily 3:25–5pm | stop: San Lazzaro*

TORCELLO
(131 E3) *(⌦ 0)*

Here, in the midst of the swamps of the lagoon, around 40 minutes north-east of the city by *vaporetto*, was one of the birthplaces of Venice's history. In the early Middle Ages, around 20,000 people lived here and Torcello was even an episcopal see. Today, the island is al-

most deserted and a popular destination for the melancholy-minded – and art enthusiasts. The more than 1,000-year-old *Santa Maria Assunta Cathedral (daily 10:30am–6pm; in winter until 5pm)* has magnificent Byzantine mosaics and the *Museo della Provincia (Tue–Sun 10:30am–5:30pm; in winter 10am–5pm)* displays priceless objects from Torcello's golden age and Roman times. The *Locanda Cipriani (closed Tue | tel. 0 41 73 01 50 | www.locandacipriani. com | Expensive)* on the main canal is a popular destination for gourmets. *Stop: Torcello*

On San Lazzaro degli Armeni: the library in the Mekhitarist monastery

FOOD & DRINK

Many people think that the *cucina veneziana*, with its traditional, exquisite recipes, is still one of the finest cuisines on earth, but there are others who feel that it has been spoiled by mass tourism.

Of course, the admirers and the moaners are both right in a way. There are still many chefs who create wonderful dishes to tickle the diner's palate using the great variety of freshly-caught seafood from the Adriatic and fresh, crisp produce from the "vegetable islands" and mainland, but you will equally well find the mass-produced *menu turistico* at a set price – and often, not a very reasonable one at that – served up like a dog's dinner. In any case, the Venetian cuisine still has many incomparable specialities, ranging from the dozens of different varieties of pasta to the imaginative *frutti di mare* and meat dishes and sweet delights from the cake shops.

Those who want to experience everything the gastronomic landscape of the city has to offer, should start off by going to a few *bacari* (with the stress on the first "a"). These simple stand-up bars are the Venetian equivalent of the Spanish tapas bar, the Parisian bistro or the local pub in Britain – an institution, where you can have a glass of wine, an *ombra*, nibble a couple of delicious snacks, the *cicheti*, and – first and foremost – have a chat.

Regardless of whether you eat in a gourmet restaurant or trattoria, the classical menu is always the same: you begin with starters *(antipasti)*, followed by soup,

Enjoy the cuisine of the lagoon in countless *trattorias*, *bacari* and gourmet restaurants in the city

pasta or risotto as the *primo piatto* (first course). The main course *(secondo piatto)* consists of fish or meat with a vegetable or salad side dish *(contorno)*, which must be ordered separately. All of this comes to an end with a dessert *(dolce)* and/or fruit. This is usually accompanied by wine *(vino)*, often the house wine *(della casa)* with a carafe of water to quench your thirst.

The kitchens are usually open from noon until around 2:30pm for lunch, and from 7pm to around 10pm in the evening.

There is almost always an extra cover charge *(pane e coperta)* of 1–3 euros (sometimes more); this includes bread to go with your meal. It will say on the menu if the service charge *(servizio)* is included; if not, a tip of five to ten percent is appropriate – as long as you were satisfied.

BACARI, BARS & OSTERIAS

Locals usually gather in these generally simply furnished, but extremely cosy wine

Sushi and Sashimi in Naranzaria made with fresh fish from the market next door

bars to have a chat with their neighbours – usually standing up, to eat a few tasty titbits (in the case of the osteria, this is a real meal seated at a table) and knock back an *ombra*, a small glass of white wine that is impossible to imagine Venetian life without.

ACIUGHETA
(127 D2–3) (*L7*)

A fine selection of *cicheti*, pizzas and other delicious things, as well as good wines, just a few yards behind St Mark's Basilica. Soak up the atmosphere at one of the tables outside if the weather is fine. *Daily (sometimes closed Wed in winter) | Campo Santi Filippo e Giacomo 4357 | tel. 04 15 22 42 92 | stop: San Zaccaria*

INSIDER TIP DA ALBERTO
(123 D6) (*L5*)

Fans of excellent fish – come right in! There is a different menu every day which includes specialities such as spaghetti with scampi or squid, fish gnocchi or risotto, dried cod in salt, and much more. *Daily |* Calle Ciacinto Gallina 5401 | tel. 04 15 23 81 53 | www.osteriadaalberto.it | stop: Ospedale

AMERICAN BAR (126 C3) (*K7*)

Although you can't sit down, the location right below the clock tower on St Mark's Square is unbeatable, the selection of sandwiches and drinks is excellent and the prices – especially compared to the wickedly expensive posh cafés in the area – are pleasantly moderate. Plus, you can still enjoy the unique panorama of the square at the standing tables outside. *Daily | stop: San Marco*

ANTICO CALICE (126 C1) (*J6*)

Located right around the corner from the lively Campo San Bartolomeo, this storybook Osteria serves up an incredible selection of classic specialities and good wines to a mixed crowd of young locals and tourists in equal measure. *Daily | Calle degli Stagneri 5228 | tel. 04 15 20 97 75 | anticocalice.it | stop: Rialto*

INSIDER TIP AI ASSASSINI
(126 A3) (∅ H7)

The patron of this inviting osteria, Giuseppe Galardi, whips up different daily specials including poultry and red meat (Mon/Tue), *bollito misto* (Wed), stockfish (Thu) and seafood (Fri). Delicious wines and *cicheti* are served at the bar. *Closed Sun | Rio Terrà degli Assassini 3695 | tel. 04 15 28 79 86 | www.osteriaaiassassini. it | stop: Sant'Angelo*

DO MORI ★
(122 B6) (∅ H5–6)

This is the oldest *bacaro* in Venice and has been here near the fish market for over 500 years. Countless pots and copper kettles hang from the ceiling and more than 100 different wines await you at the bar. All of this with many kinds of *tramezzini* and other snacks. *Closed Sun and after 7:30pm | Calle dei Do Mori 429 | tel. 04 15 22 54 01 | stop: Rialto*

INSIDER TIP AL MERCÀ
(122 B6) (∅ J5)

A pick-me-up, standing in the open air on a peaceful square near Rialto Bridge: tasty unusual canapés with horsemeat, cauliflower, dried cod or tuna… Good local wine. *Closed Sun | Fondamenta Riva Olio 213 | tel. 0 39 92 47 81 | stop: Rialto*

NARANZARIA ★
(122 B6) (∅ J5)

This classy pub in the new trendy quarter between the fish market and Rialto Bridge serves spicy snacks as well as main dishes ranging from *carpaccio* to couscous, from polenta to pasta, and even sushi, accompanied by excellent wines from Friuli. If the weather is fine, you can sit outside on the Canal Grande until long past midnight. *Nov–March closed Mon | Fondamenta Riva Olio 130 | tel. 04 17 24 10 35 | www.naranzaria.it | stop: Rialto*

AI PROMESSI SPOSI
(122 B5) (∅ J5)

This is the place to taste savoury snacks and a great variety of fish dishes at the bar. *Closed Wed | Calle dell'Oca 4367 | tel. 04 12 41 27 47 | stop: Ca' d'Oro*

LA RIVISTA
(125 E5) (∅ F9)

Stylish wine-and-cheese bar in the cellar of the design hotel Ca' Pisani. Tasty cold food and small warm dishes, excellent range of wines; drinks in the Rivista's bar. *Closed Mon | Rio Terrà Foscarini 979 | tel. 04 12 40 14 25 | stops: Accademia, Zattere*

RUGA RIALTO
(126 A1) (∅ H6)

Tasty, traditional food in cosy surroundings served to a – mainly young – artistic

---

MARCO POLO HIGHLIGHTS

★ **Do Mori**
You should treat yourself to a glass of wine in Venice's oldest wine bar → p. 63

★ **Naranzaria**
In this gourmet restaurant, it is possible to sit directly on the Canal Grande until late at night → p. 63

★ **Florian**
The oldest café in Venice → p. 65

★ **Corte Sconta**
Wonderful fish dishes → p. 65

★ **Da Romano**
A real feast on Burano → p. 67

crowd. *Daily | Ruga Vecchia San Giovanni (alias Ruga Rialto) 692 | tel. 04 15 21 12 43 | stop: Rialto*

DO SPADE
(122 A6) *(ℳ H5)*

Traditional Venetian cuisine and exceptional local wines are served in the cosy, wood-panelled rooms. *Daily | Calle Do Spade 860 | tel. 04 15 21 05 83 | stop: Rialto*

INSIDER TIP ▶ ALASKA
(121 D5) *(ℳ F5)*

This is far the most unusual – and probably the smallest – *gelateria* in the city. Carlo Pistacchi makes dozens of exotic and unusual types of ice cream from natural ingredients, ranging from as-

From a pub to gourmet restaurant: Da Fiore

TEAMO
(126 A2) *(ℳ H7)*

Delectable delicacies in a stylish ambiance – great for a tasty snack or a good chat with an excellent glass of wine or a cocktail. Tip: the mixed *cicheti* platter. *Closed Tue | Rio Terà della Mandola 3795 | tel. 04 15 28 37 87 | stop: Sant'Angelo*

VECIO FRITOLIN (118 A5) *(ℳ H5)*

Very traditional osteria, full of atmosphere, perfect for a good meal or just a few savoury *cicheti*. *Closed Mon and Tue evening | Calle della Regina, 2262 | tel. 04 15 22 28 81 | stop: San Stae*

paragus and ginger or artichoke and liquorice to mulberry. Pure poetry! *Daily 11am–11pm; in winter noon–10pm, closed Dec/Jan | Calle Larga dei Bari 1159 | stops: Ferrovia, Riva di Biasio*

CAFFÈ DEL DOGE (126 B1) *(ℳ J6)*

Coffee aficionados will feel they are in paradise here not far from Rialto Bridge: dozens of different kinds of freshly roasted beans for you to try. Knowledgeable staff and sweet treats. *Mon–Sat 7am–7pm, Sun (except July/Aug) 7am–1pm | Calle dei Cinque 609 | stops: San Silvestro, Rialto*

FLORIAN ⭐ ☝
(126 C3) (⌖ K8)

Praising this almost 300-year-old noble establishment would be like carrying coals to Newcastle. A cappuccino in its elegant rooms with their panelling and mirrors, or outside on the Piazza San Marco to the strains of the salon orchestra in the background, is part of the standard *grand tour* programme – in spite of the really steep prices. A word of warning: if you sit outside, you will be charged an extra 5.80 euros for the music (in the Café Quadri across the square, it is 4.80 euros!). *Daily 9am–midnight; in winter until 11pm | Piazza San Marco 56 | www.caffe-florian.com | stop: San Marco*

ZANSIBAR
(127 D1) (⌖ K6)

This is something like a beach bar on one of the most atmospheric squares in the *centro storico*. Pizza, sandwiches, hotdogs, hamburgers, *gelati*, beer and plenty of high spirits. *Tue–Sun 7am–1am | Campo Santa Maria Formosa 5840 | stops: Rialto, San Zaccaria*

RESTAURANTS: EXPENSIVE

CORTE SCONTA ⭐
(128 A3) (⌖ N8)

This modestly furnished restaurant is not easy to find but you will be rewarded with an excellent selection of first-class fish. It

GOURMET RESTAURANTS

Da Fiore (125 F1) (⌖ G5)
Mara and Maurizio Martin have transformed what was once a simple hostelry into an exquisite restaurant. The fish, risotto, desserts and great variety of rare cheese have become famous. *From 75 euros | closed Sun/Mon | Calle del Scaleter 2202 | tel. 0 41 72 13 08 | stops: San Stae, San Silvestro*

Harry's Bar (126 B4) (⌖ J8)
Those who are admirers of legendary locations will just have to go up to the first floor and try the *carpaccio*, the legendary starter created decades ago by the owner. Ernest Hemingway, Maria Callas, Humphrey Bogart: they are all immortalised in the valuable leather-bound guest book. In case the prices appear much too high, and that would not come as a surprise, you can try a Bellini, Cipriani's famous prosecco and peach drink, in the bar and soak up the atmosphere. *From*

70 euros | daily | Calle Vallaresso 1323 | tel. 04 15 28 57 77 | stop: Vallaresso

Da Ivo (126 B3) (⌖ J7)
Don't be fooled by the rather rustic appearance: this restaurant is famous for its exquisite Tuscan-Venetian cuisine. Speciality: fish and meat grilled over charcoal. Hundreds of bottles of the very best wines are stored in the cellar. *From 70 euros | closed Sun | Ramo dei Fuseri 1809 | tel. 04 15 28 50 04 | stops: Rialto, Vallaresso*

Quadri ☝ (126 C3) (⌖ K7)
The famous café on Pizza San Marco also has an extremely elegant restaurant on the first floor. The view of the square is phenomenal; the cuisine will satisfy the most demanding guests. The palace-like atmosphere will take you back to the 19th century. *From 75 euros | closed Mon from Nov–March | Piazza San Marco 120 | tel. 04 15 22 21 05 | stop: San Marco*

takes some time to get used to the fact that the specials of the day are not listed on the menu but rattled off by the lady of the house in Italian. Our tip: trust the chef and order an opulent plate of antipasti. But, be careful: quality has a price! *Closed Sun/Mon | Calle del Pestrin 3886 | tel. 04 15 22 70 24 | www.cortescontave nezia.it | stop: Arsenale*

INSIDER TIP ▶ IL RIDOTTO
(127 D2) (*ØJ L7*)

This restaurant, with its brick walls and mirrors and minimalistic, elegant atmosphere, only has enough room for a maximum of 13 guests. It is therefore not surprising that you need to reserve well in advance and that Gianni Bonacorsi charges 5 euros for the *coperto*. In return, he serves his guests culinary highlights of supreme quality. Of course, there is pasta

and rice served with amazing wines every day; the meat, fish and other exquisite ingredients vary with what the market supplies. *Closed Thu at noon and Wed | Campo Santi Filippo e Giacomo 4509 | tel. 04 15 20 82 80 | www.ilridotto.com | stop: San Zaccaria*

LA RIVIERA
(124 C5) (*ØJ D9*)

At the western end of the Zattere, the owners Monica and Luca pamper their guests in cosy surroundings, with excellent cooking and fine wines. It is especially delightful eating outside on a sunny day with a view of Giudecca across the wide canal. *Closed Mon | Fondamenta Zattere al Ponte Lungo 1473 | tel. 04 15 22 76 21 | www.ristoranteriviera.it | stop: San Basilio*

RESTAURANTS: MODERATE

ANDRI
(131 D4)

In his chic trattoria on the Lido, Luca Menighetti likes to serve tastily prepared fish – and the large-sized, colourful paintings he has painted are also a feast for the eyes. The mixed antipasti and fish risotto are especially recommendable. *Closed Mon/Tue | Via Lepanto 21 | tel. 04 15 26 54 82 | stop: Lido*

ANTICA BIRRARIA LA CORTE
(125 F1) (*ØJ G6*)

This restaurant in a former brewery on the idyllic Campo San Polo is a good place to have a tasty, low-brow lunch or dinner. The high-ceilinged narrow rooms and covered courtyard are cool and chic with high-quality professionalism reigning in the kitchen. Specialities, grilled chicken, veal and horsemeat. Many people like to have their aperitif outside at one of the tables on the square. *Daily | Campo San*

LOW BUDGET

The *Cea* (123 K4–5) (*ØJ L4*) *(closed Sat evening and Sun | Campiello del Pestrin 5422a | tel. 04 15 23 74 50 | stop: Fondamenta Nuove)* is a simple, friendly trattoria with tables outside and very reasonably-priced risottos, pizzas and fish.

The prices are very affordable at the *Caffè Letterario* (127 D2) (*ØJ L6*) *(Tue–Sun 10am–7pm| Campo Santa Maria Formosa 5252 | tel. stop: San Zaccaria)* on the ground floor of the Fondazione Querini Stampalia, which is a popular meeting place for art students and clerical workers.

Polo 2168 | tel. 04 12 75 05 70 | www.birrarialacorte.it | stop: San Silvestro

LINEA D'OMBRA
(126 A5) (*ᗕ H10*)

Creative cooking focussing on sophisticated fish dishes and a list of more than 600 (!) wines draw people to this smartly designed restaurant at the eastern end

FIASCHETTERIA TOSCANA
(122 C6) (*ᗕ J5*)

There are not many other places in Venice where you can eat as well as here. From risotto to zabaione, from the perfectly grilled steak to the fried fish, the chef really shows that he is an artist. The atmosphere is tasteful but not ostentatious, the prices not low but justified. *Closed*

It is worth taking the boat to Burano to eat at Da Romano

of the Zattere. Unforgettable: a meal on the wooden pontoon terrace directly over the water. *Closed Wed | Zattere/Ponte dell'Unita 19 | tel. 04 12 41 18 81 | www.ristorantelineadombra.com | stop: Salute*

DA ROMANO ★
(131 E3) (*ᗕ X2*)

For generations, Venetian gourmands and gourmets have travelled over to Burano to eat in this trattoria that is famous far and near. The splendid cuisine focuses on fish that is cooked here with great care over a charcoal fire. *Closed Sun evening and Tue in summer, every evening in winter | Via Baldassarre Galuppi 221 | tel. 0 41 73 00 30 | www.daromano.it | stop: Burano*

Wed lunchtime and Tue | Salizada San Giovanni Crisostomo 5719 | tel. 04 15 28 52 81 | www.fiaschetteriatoscana.it | stop: Rialto

INSIDER TIP ▶ ALLA VECCHIA PESCHERIA ⊛ (131 D3) (*ᗕ Q3*)

An old factory warehouse on Murano decorated with stylish furnishings and contemporary art. Picturesque terrace with a fountain. The menu features creative gourmet dishes made from local organic products farmed on the nearby vegetable islands as well as fresh fish and dolce *alla mamma. Closed Wed | Campiello Pescheria 4 | tel. 04 15 27 49 57 | www.allavecchiapescheria.com | stop: Colonna*

LOCAL SPECIALITIES

baccalà mantecato – a paste made of mashed dried cod, garlic, onions and olive oil that is often spread on toast or slices of polenta (photo left)

bigoli in salsa – spaghetti with anchovy sauce

carpaccio – Venice's culinary export hit: wafer-thin slices of raw beef, with a trickle of lemon juice and flakes of Parmesan

cicheti – Venetian-style tapas: titbits such as small meatballs, tiny fried fish, pickled vegetables, mussels, stuffed olives, slices of polenta, etc. (photo right)

fegato alla venexiana – calf's liver cooked in a white-wine-and-onion stock

fiori di zucca – pumpkin flowers, usually served stuffed and fried

fritto misto di mare – fried fish and seafood

pasta e fagioli – a substantial stew cooked with thick macaroni, white beans and a lot of olive oil and herbs

risi e bisi – rice with green peas

risotto nero – creamy, black risotto prepared with squid ink *(seppie)*

sarde in soar – a very traditional, very Venetian, starter: cooked sardines served cold with a marinade of olive oil, vinegar, wine, raisins and pine nuts

tramezzini – triangular crust-less sandwiches with cheese, ham, mushrooms, tuna, egg or vegetables and various spreads

INSIDER TIP ▶ **VINI DA GIGIO**
(122 B4) (*J4*)
Excellent cooking that concentrates on seasonal products. And this, in pleasant, cultivated, unpretentious surroundings and prices that represent fairly reasonable value for money. That also appeals to locals – so reserve in advance! *Closed Mon/Tue* | *Fondamenta San Felice 3628a* | *tel. 04 15 28 51 40* | *www.vinidagigio.com* | *stop: Ca' d'Oro*

RESTAURANTS: BUDGET

ALL'ANTICA MOLA
(121 E2) (*G2*)
A simple, but homey trattoria with hearty, typically Venetian food. On fine days you

can sit outside: either in the little garden behind the building or directly on the canal. Hot dishes from morning to late at night! *Closed Wed | Fondamenta degli Ormesini 2800 | tel. 0 41 71 74 92 | stop: Guglie*

BANDIERETTE
(123 E6) *(ω M6)*

Good, home-style cooking – something that sounds as simple as that is almost a rarity in Venice these days. At noon, local workers drop in and choose from the two or three *primi* and *secondi* of the day. In the evening, the fare is a bit more up-market. No wonder that it will be hard to find a table if you haven't reserved. *Closed Mon evening and Tue | Barbaria de le Tole 6671 | tel. 04 15 22 06 19 | stop: Ospedale*

LE CAMPANE
(121 E3–4) *(ω F3)*

This respectable, family-run trattoria with a large garden near the railway station specialises in fish. *Daily | Rio Terà San Leonardo 1401 | tel. 0 41 71 83 45 | stop: Guglie*

INSIDER TIP BACARANDO AI CORAZZIERI
(127 F3) *(ω N7)*

Cosy trattoria with a lovely covered summer terrace on Campo Bandiera e Moro. A nice, family-run place serving a variety of meat and fish dishes as well as delicious home-made desserts. Live jazz music once or twice a week. *Daily | Salizada del Pignater 3839 | tel. 04 15 28 98 59 | bacarando.com | stop: Arsenale*

DOGE MOROSINI
(125 F4) *(ω G8)*

Centrally-located, well-managed osteria. The service is friendly and exceedingly efficient, the cooking superb – and that, with large portions and at low prices. The menu changes daily and includes five *primi* and *secondi*. *Closed Mon | Campo Santo Stefano 2958 | www.osteriado gemorosini.it | tel. 04 15 22 69 22 | stop: Accademia*

INSIDER TIP DUE COLONNE
(121 E6) *(ω G5)*

Those in the know say that this is probably the best pizzeria in town. Venetian *sfiaceti* with ham and horsemeat are also a speciality. *Closed Mon | Campo Sant'Agostin 2343 | tel. 04 17 17338 | stops: San Silvestro, San Stae*

INSIDER TIP FANTÀSIA
(127 F3) *(ω N8)*

Good, typical Venetian cuisine with a strong dose of social responsibility. When you order the delicious pasta, pizzas, risotti or fish dishes here, you are supporting a charity organization that helps people with disabilities. *Closed Mon | Calle Pestrin Castello 3911 | tel. 04 15 22 80 38 | www.uniamogoldin.it | stop: Arsenale*

GAM-GAM
(121 E3) *(ω F3)*

Kosher cooking in the Jewish-Italian tradition: falafel, gefilte fish and other oriental-style recipes accompanied by excellent Israeli wines. *Closed Fri evening and Sat | Sotoportego del Gheto Vecchio 1122 | tel. 04 12 75 92 56 | www.gamgamkosher.com | stop: Guglie*

GIORGIONE
(128 C4) *(ω O9)*

Popular meeting place for the locals who are full of praise for Signora Ivana's fish dishes and also love to listen to Signore Lucio Bisutto singing folksongs in the evening. Here, even the menu turistico is good! *Closed Wed | Via Garibaldi 1533 | tel. 04 15 22 87 27 | www.ristorantegior gione.it | stops: Giardini, Arsenale*

SHOPPING

CITY
WHERE TO START?
The most expensive spot – and, of course, a feast for the eyes – are the boutiques in the **Mercerie**, the narrow rows of shops between Piazza San Marco and Rialto Bridge, as well as along **Calle Larga XXIII Marzo**. Things are less expensive, and there is an especially good range of textiles and leather goods, on the streets to the west of Rialto Bridge, along the streets to Campo San Polo, as well as **Lista di Spagna** and **Strada Nova.** Those looking for unusual, imaginative artistic handcrafts should wander through the side streets in the San Polo and Dorsoduro districts.

Venice is quite an expensive spot. This is particularly true of the branded articles of the global accessory and fashion industry whose dazzling boutiques in the arcades on Piazza San Marco, Mercerie and the streets parallel to them between Rialto and St Mark's Square will tempt all of those strolling through the city.

At least leather goods are still cheaper in Venice than north of the Alps. But, the traditional local products make much more interesting souvenirs – lace, hand-printed fabrics, old glass beads, hand-dipped and marbled paper, gilded picture frames and all other kinds of artistic handwork. Those looking for classical reminders of Venice will not be able to resist taking a carnival mask or vase or

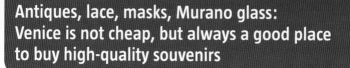

Antiques, lace, masks, Murano glass:
Venice is not cheap, but always a good place
to buy high-quality souvenirs

bowl of Murano glass back home with them. Culinary specialities, such as cheese or ham, wine, vinegar, oil or special cakes and noodles can also be recommended. There is a lot of junk and kitsch, but it is possible to find first-rate articles.

Opening hours are adjusted to the local lifestyle: on working days (including Saturday), the shops usually open their doors some time between 9am and 9:30am and close at around 12:30 or 1pm for a siesta lasting about three hours; they then stay open until 7pm or 7:30pm. Several shops remain closed on Monday morning.

DELICATESSEN

ALIANI ★
(122 B6) (*ⁿ* H6)

This classical delicatessen shop is a paradise for lovers of cheese, as well as sausages, ham and smoked meats. *Mon–Wed only am | Fondamenta Riva Olio 214 | stop: Rialto Mercato*

MAURO EL FORNER DE CANTON
(122 B5) (*ØⱮ H6*)

Biscotti, bruschette, brigiolini, grissini, dolci, pan dei dogi ("doge's bread", a kind of biscuit with hazelnuts)... a great variety of sweet and savoury baked goods. *Ruga Vecchia San Giovanni 603 | www.elfornerdecanton.com | stop: San Silvestro*

INSIDER**TIP** ▶ GIULIANA LONGO
(126 B1) (*ØⱮ J6*)

Charming hat shop over 100 years old with a large selection for men and women. *Calle del Lovo 4813 | www.giulianlongo.com | stop: Rialto*

You should make sure you're not hungry when you shop at Rizzo

RIZZO
(121 F4) (*ØⱮ G3*)

Venice's culinary traditions are still alive and well here. Gigantic selection of special noodles – from lasagne to pasta that is shaped like little gondolas... Pastries and sweets, as well as cheese, sausages, ham, wine and oil. Friendly staff behind the counter. *Rio Terà della Maddalena 1356 | www.rizzovenezia.it | stop: San Marcuola*

INSIDER**TIP** ▶ MALEFATTE ☯
(125 F4) (*ØⱮ G8*)

Shopping and social assistance all rolled into one. High-quality organic cosmetics, notepads, t-shirts and all sorts of original bags made by the inmates of the municipal prison are sold by a charitable cooperative at a kiosk on Campo Santo Stefano (or online: *www.malefatte.org*). *Mon–Sat 2pm–7pm | stop: Accademia*

GLASS

CENEDESE ⭐
(126 C3) (*∅ K8*)

Cenedese is one of the market leaders for people looking for high-quality, original pieces. *Piazza San Marco 40/41 | www.arscenedese.com | stops: San Marco, Vallaresso*

GAMBARO & POGGI
(131 D3) (*∅ Q2*)

For more than a quarter of a century, Mario Gambaro and Bruno Poggi have given full rein to their creativity. The result: vases, jugs, glasses, chandeliers... 1,300 different articles in 85 colours that you can admire, and buy, here. *Calle del Cimitero 15 | Murano | www.gambaroepoggiglass.com | stop: Venier*

GLASSES

MICROMEGA
(126 A4) (*∅ H8*)

Fantastic eyeglasses crafted in-house - chic, simple and ultra-light frames made of gold, titanium or horn. *Calle delle Ostreghe 2436 | www.micromegaottica.com | Anleger: Giglio*

INTERIOR DECORATION & ACCESSORIES

ANGELO DALLA VENEZIA
(125 F1) (*∅ G5*)

Artistically turned vases, candlesticks, fountain pens, etc.. made of precious wood. *Calle del Scaleter 2204 | stop: San Silvestro*

INSIDER TIP CAPRICCI VENEZIANI
(125 D4) (*∅ F8*)

Lovingly painted, miniature reproductions of churches, palaces and even entire districts, true to the original, made out of a mixture of resin and marble powder. Large

selection: *www.morogiovanni.com. Calle della Toletta 1193 | www.morogiovanni.com | stop: Accademia*

INSIDER TIP FRANCO FURLANETTO
(125 E2) (*∅ G6*)

A souvenir like a modern sculpture: *forcole* (oarlocks) for gondolieri made of nut or cherry wood – either full-size or as a model, from 100 euros. *Calle dei Nomboli 2768b | stop: San Tomà*

MADERA
(125 D4) (*∅ E8*)

With everything from night-table lamps, tableware, scarves and handbags to unique jewellery, three architects have created a treasure trove of household goods and fashion accessories made of wood, metal and ceramic crafted by young designers. *Campo San Barnaba 2762 and Calle Lunga San Barnaba 2729 | www.maderavenezia.it | stop: Ca' Rezzonico*

⭐ **Aliani**
A dream for all cheese, sausage and ham fans → p. 71

⭐ **Cenedese**
Superlative Murano glass right on the Piazza San Marco → p. 73

⭐ **Legatoria Piazzesi**
Hand-dipped paper of the highest quality → p. 75

⭐ **Venetia Studium**
Exquisite plissé fabrics and silk lamps → p. 74

⭐ **Signor Blum**
3-D wooden puzzles as souvenirs → p. 75

MARCO POLO HIGHLIGHTS

creations. *Calle del Scaletter 2236 | labe rintho.it | stop: San Silvestro*

ANNELIE
(125 D4) *(𝄞 E8)*
Bed linen and tablecloths, as well as baby-wear, curtains and shirts, etc., decorated with embroidery or fine lace. *Calle Lunga San Barnaba 2748 | stop: Ca' Rezzonico*

ARRAS
(125 D3) *(𝄞 F7)*
A large selection of colourful, hand-woven silk, woollen and cotton fabrics. *Campiello Squellini 3235 | stop: Ca' Rezzonico*

GAGGIO **(125 F3)** *(𝄞 G8)*
Emma Gaggio's exquisite, hand-printed velvet is used to make cushions, bags, scarves, hats and many other articles. *Calle delle Botteghe 3451 | stop: Sant'Angelo*

MASKS

INSIDER TIP ▶ **CA' MACANA** ●
(125 D4) *(𝄞 E8)*
This quality producer, with two shops in Dorsoduro, also offers courses in his studio where groups or individual tourists are given a theoretical and practical introduction to the art of mask-making. Showrooms: *Fondamenta Rezzonico 3172 and Fondamenta Lombardo 1169 | www. camacana.com | stop: Ca' Rezzonico*

Three other mask producers are much more creative than the mass of suppliers: *Tragicomica* **(125 E2)** *(𝄞 G6)* *(Calle dei Nomboli 2800 | stop: San Tomà); Mistero Buffo* **(124 B4)** *(𝄞 D9) (Fondamenta San Basilio 1645 | stop: San Basilio); Marega* **(127 E2)** *(𝄞 L7) (Fondamenta dell'Osmarin 4968 and 4976a | stop: San Zaccaria)*

Venetia Studium: in the spirit of Mariano Fortuny

VENETIA STUDIUM ★
(126 A–B4) *(𝄞 H8)*
Clothes and fabrics, hand-painted silk lamps, furnishings designed by Mariano Fortuny. Several branches, including *Calle Larga XXIII Marzo 2425 | www.venetia studium.com | stop: Vallaresso*

JEWELLERY

COSTANTINI **(131 D3)** *(𝄞 Q2)*
Traditional beads and fashionable jewellery - high quality and made of glass. *Calle del Cimitero 11 | Murano | www.cos tantiniglassbeads.com | stop: Venier*

LABERINTHO **(125 F1)** *(𝄞 G5)*
Several young goldsmiths have joined forces here to present their imaginative

PAPER

INSIDER TIP ▶ EBRÙ
(125 F4) *(⨂ G8)*

Alberto Valese was one of the pioneers in the marble-paper boom of the 1980s and has remained one of the masters of the craft until today. He not only offers the entire range of this type of product – hand-dipped papers, book bindings and various decorative objects – but also regular courses in intimate surroundings. Participants find out a great deal about the centuries-old tradition of his art and also learn how to make dyes and materials themselves as well as marble paper. *Campo Santo Stefano 3471 | www.albertovalese-ebru.it | stops: San Samuele, Sant'Angelo*

LEGATORIA PIAZZESI ⭐
(126 A4) *(⨂ H8)*

The last of its kind: here, printing is still carried out the old-fashioned way using wooden blocks. The selection of paper, cards and greetings cards – some of them hand-dipped – is a feast for the eyes. *Campo Santa Maria del Giglio 2511c | stop: Giglio*

SHOES & LEATHERWEAR

BRUNO MAGLI (126 B3) *(⨂ J8)*

Classic chic: shoes from leading Italian designers, practically tailor-made. *Calle dell'Ascensione 1302 | stop: Vallaresso*

INSIDER TIP ▶ PIEDÀTERRE
(122 B6) *(⨂ J6)*

The soft-as-silk slippers *(furlane)* with their non-slip rubber soles that the gondolieri wear when they are working used to be available in many shops. Today, cheap reproductions from the Far East have flooded the market. But here you will still find the original – of linen, with or without silk ribbons in all kinds of bright colours. Price from 32 euros for a pair. *Ruga degli Oresi 60 | stop: Rialto*

ROSSETTI (126 B3) *(⨂ J8)*

A treasure trove for admirers of fashionable footwear. *Salizada San Moisè 1477 | stop: Vallaresso*

TOYS

INSIDER TIP ▶ GILBERTO PENZO
(125 E2) *(⨂ G6)*

Delightful models of Venetian watercraft. You can also buy do-it-yourself gondola model kits; prices start at 25 euros. *Calle Seconda dei Saoneri 2681 | www.veniceboats.com | stop: San Tomà*

SIGNOR BLUM ⭐ (125 D4) *(⨂ E8)*

Three-dimensional, hand-sawn, unmistakably Venetian, wooden puzzles – a tasteful present! *Campo San Barnaba 2840 | stop: Ca' Rezzonico*

LOW BUDGET

Fish, fruit, vegetables and spices are usually much cheaper at the small markets, e.g. *Campo Santa Margherita* **(125 D3)** *(⨂ E7)* or *Rio Terà San Leonardo* **(121 E4)** *(⨂ G3)* (both *Mon–Sat 8am–2pm)* than in shops.

Chic, reasonably-priced dresses, jackets, bags and many more articles made of silk, velvet and brocade, tailored by the female inmates of the Giudecca Prison, make a visit to ⓦ *Banco No. 10* **(127 F2–3)** *(⨂ M7)* *(Salizada Sant'Antonin 3478a | stop: San Zaccaria)* worthwhile. Each piece is unique and also helps the prisoners' rehabilitation programme.

ENTERTAINMENT

CITY **WHERE TO START?**

You will find the best selection of bars, pubs, artists'
cafés – some of them with live
performances – around the
Campi Santa Margherita and
San Pantalon, as well as along
the wide **canals in Cannaregio**. Other popular stomping
grounds are the squares **south-
east of Rialto Bridge**, such as
San Bartolomeo, San Luca and
San Lio. It is much more tranquil in the alfresco bars along
the ● Canal Grande near the
Fabbriche Vecchie – especially
on balmy summer nights.

Thank goodness the time when all Venice
went to bed long before midnight is long
past. Today a varied club, bar and theatre
scene keeps many parts of the city well
and truly awake until early in the morning. In addition, there are festive musical
performances every evening at La Fenice
Opera House and in the theatres and
palaces.

Especially in the summer months from
March to October and during the carnival
season, La Serenissima delights its guests
with an extensive programme of evening
events offering more than you would
consider possible in a small town with a
population of only 60,000. That is when
regular concerts which are well-worth
hearing are held in numerous *palazzi*,
churches and *scuole*. There are also sev-

A lively bar and pub scene: nightlife pulsates on the streets and squares of Venice

eral theatres, cabarets and cinemas offering excellent performances – if your Italian is up to it.

The sumptuous productions and excellent casts of the Teatro Fenice have earned it a fine reputation as one of the leading opera houses in Italy. The famous casino and many discotheques are open until late at night. But, most importantly, a lively bar and pub scene has developed in recent years and provides many possibilities to get a feeling for local colour surrounded by young Venetians and guest students until well past midnight.

There are often live concerts and sometimes also street art in the evening on *campi Santa Maria Formosa, Santa Margherita, Pisani, Angelo Raffaele, San Barnaba* and *Santi Giovanni e Paolo*. For up-to-date information see *www.aguestinvenice.com*, *www.venezianews.it*, *www.veneziasi.it* and *www.meetingvenice.it*, as well as the (Italian/English) magazines "INVenice" and "Venezia News" and the official calendar of events published in a free pamphlet.

CASINO

Today, you can try your luck behind the ● impressive façade of the *Palazzo Vendramin-Calergi* (121 F4) (*M G4*) on the Canal Grande where Richard Wagner wrote "Parsifal". Roulette, blackjack, gaming machines, etc. *Daily 3:30pm– 2:45 am | www.casinovenezia.it | stop: San Marcuola*

original version with Italian subtitles. *Salizada San Stae 1990 | tel. 04 15 24 13 20 | stop: San Stae*

CONCERTS

COLLEGIUM DUCALE

This chamber orchestra was founded in 1993 and now gives several concerts a week of a high standard with music from

The Centrale is bar, lounge and restaurant all rolled into one

CINEMA

Most of the films shown in the few remaining cinemas in Venice have been synchronised into Italian but there is one exception:

INSIDER TIP ► CASA DEL CINEMA
(121 F5) (*M G5*)

This meeting place for cineastes next to the Palazzo Mocenigo shows high-quality films from all over the world, partly in the

the Baroque, Classical and Romantic periods. The performances alternate between *Palazzo delle Prigioni* (127 D3) (*M L8*) to the east of the Doge's Palace and the "Blue Room" at the *Teatro San Gallo* (126 B3) (*M J7*). *Tel. 0 41 98 81 55 | www.collegiumducale.com*

INTERPRETI VENEZIANI ★ ●
(125 F4) (*M G8*)

This chamber music group gives splendid concerts entitled "Violins in Venice" on more than 200 days of the year in the former San Vidal Church. The highlights of the programme include works by Bach, Vivaldi, Tartini & co. *Tel. 04 12 77 05 61 | www.interpretiveneziani.com*

VIRTUOSI DI VENEZIA
(126 C2–3) (*⑳ K7*)
Baroque orchestral music hits, ranging from Vivaldi's "Four Seasons" to Albinoni's Adagio – as well as arias by Mozart, Verdi and Donizetti. Dressed in period costume, the Virtuosi di Venezia give several concerts of opera and orchestral classics weekly in the *Ateneo di San Basso* behind St Mark's Basilica. *Piazzetta dei Leoni | tel. 04 15 28 28 25 | www.virtuo sidivenezia.com*

DISCOTHEQUES & BEACH PARTIES

On warm summer evenings, take the night *vaporetto* (line N) from San Zaccaria to the Lido to dance the night away at one of the beach discos. The trendy addresses at the moment are: *Blue Beach (Wed, Fri, Sat 9am–2am, Mon, Tue, Thu, Sun 9am–9pm | Lungomare Gabriele D'Annunzio 20),* as a fish restaurant as well as a bar, there's the *Pagoda Des Bains (daily 10am–2am | Lungomare Guglielmo Marconi 23)* at the hotel of the same name and the *Pachuka (daily 9am–10pm | Viale Klinger/ Spiaggia San Nicolò).*
Unfortunately, the old town has little to offer. One address for the undaunted is *Piccolo Mondo Music & Dance* (125 E5) (*⑳ F9*) *(daily 11pm–4am | Calle Contarini Corfù 1056a | stop: Accademia),* a disco pub where people like Mick Jagger and Liza Minelli have had fun in times gone by.

PUBS, BARS, CLUBS, CAFÉS & LIVE MUSIC

ART BLU CAFFÈ (125 F4) (*⑳ G8*)
A bright and friendly eatery with a functional modern look. Best tip: the ⚡ terrace with its amazing panorama – ideal for a nightcap at the end of the day. *Daily until 11pm | Campo Santo Stefano 2808a | stop: Accademia*

BACARO JAZZ (122 C6) (*⑳ J6*)
Well-stocked cocktail bar serving food (until 2am!) with a unique and colourful ambiance. An ideal place for jazz lovers and night owls. *Daily 11am–ca.2:30am, Happy Hour 4pm–6pm | Salizada del Fondaco dei Tedeschi 5546 | stop: Rialto*

B-BAR ● (126 B4) (*⑳ J8*)
This well-known haunt in the luxury hotel The Bauer's is also popular among prominent night owls such as the likes of Daniel Craig, Al Pacino or Sting. And for good reason: the atmosphere is elegant, but intimate and the selection of creative cocktails is excellent. Plus, there is live piano music and dancing on Fri/Sat. *Campo San Moisè 1459 | tel. 04 15 20 70 22 | www.bauervenezia.com | stop: Vallaresso*

CAFÉ NOIR (125 D2) (*⑳ E–F7*)
Quirky but charming bar with a stylish interior and unusually great prices. Popu-

⭐ **Interpreti Veneziani**
Baroque music by Bach, Vivaldi & Co. in the former church of San Vidal → p. 79

⭐ **Teatro La Fenice**
Opera, dance and concerts in the oldest theatre in the city → p. 81

MARCO POLO HIGHLIGHTS

lar among students and the Happy Hour aperitivi are very inexpensive. *Mon–Sat 7am–2am, Sun 9am–2am | Calle Lunga San Pantalon 3805 | stop: San Tomà*

LOW BUDGET

The following experimental theatres and cultural meeting places offer fascinating theatre, dance, music and multi-media performances at affordable prices and the opportunity to come into contact with the young people of Venice. Some of the most interesting are: *Teatro Fondamenta Nuove* **(122 C3)** *(𝔐 K3) (Fondamenta Nuove 5013 | tel. 04 15 22 44 98 | www. teatrofondmentanuove.it | stop: Fondamenta Nuove)*, *Teatro Toniolo* **(131 D3)** *(𝔐 0) (Piazzetta Battisti 3 | tel. 0 41 97 16 66 | www.teatrotoniolo. info)* in Mestre; also in Mestre: *Centro Culturale Candiani* **(131 D3)** *(𝔐 0) (Piazzale Candiani 7 | tel. 04 12 38 61 26 | www.centroculturalecandiani.it)*

In odd years, the *Biennale for Music*, Theatre and Dance is held parallel to the art biennale during the summer months. Tickets are surprisingly reasonably priced and also allow you to see otherwise off-limits sections of the Arsenal. *Tel. 04 15 21 88 98 | www.la biennale.org*

Some of the squares have developed into trendy locations in the summer season where people, drink, chat and flirt until the early hours of the morning – first and foremost the *campi San Luca*, ● *Santa Margherita*, *San Pantalon* and ● *San Bartolomeo*.

CAFFÈ ROSSO (125 D3) *(𝔐 E7)*
Popular café among young locals with a view of one of the best squares in town. Good wines and delicious tramezini and panini. Live jazz, blues and folk music outdoors in summer. *Mon–Sat 7am–1am | Campo Santa Margherita 2963 | stop: Ca' Rezzonico*

CENTRALE (126 B3) *(𝔐 J8)*
Trendy, international class, restaurant-bar. The food is well above average; the atmosphere stylish. The music is mainly chillout-lounge and house. Rather pricey. *Wed–Mon 7pm–1am | Piscina Frezzeria 1659 | www.caffecentralevenezia.com | stop: Vallaresso*

DA CODROMA
(124 B4) *(𝔐 D8)*
On some evenings, this "in" bar with its old-fashioned furnishing is so packed with students that you can hardly move. They know that this is a good place to munch on the inexpensive *cicheti* and have a glass of fine wine. *Mon–Sat 8am–midnight | Fondamenta Briati 2540 | stop: San Basilio*

SENSO UNICO/CORNER PUB
(125 F5) *(𝔐 G9)*
An enclave of English lifestyle and an Eldorado for beer lovers. Very popular with Venetians and – mainly Anglo-Saxon – students. *Wed–Mon 10:30am–1am | Calle della Chiesa 684 | stop: Accademia*

TARNOWSKA'S AMERICAN BAR ●
(126 A4) *(𝔐 H8)*
Classic, old-school bar with an early 20th-century touch. Enjoy excellent wines, vodka and cocktails with cheese and snacks in oversized leather armchairs. *Daily 4pm–1am | Campo Santa Maria del Giglio 2494 | Hotel Ala | stop: Giglio*

TORINO@NOTTE
(126 B2) *(m J7)*

Only three minutes from Piazza San Marco: long drinks, snacks and hot music; live jam-sessions on Wed. *Tue–Sat 7pm–1am, bar open from 8am | Campo San Luca 459 | stop: Rialto*

INSIDER TIP ▶ VENICE JAZZ CLUB
(125 D4) *(m E8)*

The home of the VJC-Quartett that delights jazz fans five evenings a week with live gigs featuring classic jazz standards. Relaxed atmosphere, Happy Hour specials from 7pm, snacks. *Mon–Wed, Fr, Sa 19–1, Konzertbeginn 21 Uhr | Ponte dei Pugni 3102 | www.venicejazzclub.com | Anleger: Ca' Rezzonico*

SHOW

VENEZIA – THE SHOW
(126 A3) *(m J7)*

An elaborate multi-media spectacle: actors in historical costumes tell (in English, simultaneous translation through headphones) about Venice's more than 1,000 years of history supported by cutting-edge digital technology; the show can also be booked together with a buffet dinner. *Campo San Gallo 1097 | tel. 04 12 41 20 02 | www.teatro sangallo.net*

THEATRE & OPERA

TEATRO LA FENICE ★
(126 A3) *(m H8)*

The theatre burned to the ground in 1996 but the old "Phoenix" rose again from the ashes and was reopened in 2003 – "dov'era e com'era" where and as it was – on Campo Fantin in the form of a time-honoured, golden theatre with rows of boxes. In Venice, tickets for the excellently cast opera and dance performances, as well as concerts, are available from

A temple of the muses since 1678: Teatro Malibran

the theatre's box office and the Ve.La. ticket offices at the railway station and Piazzale Roma. Information and tickets from abroad: *tel. 04 12 42 24. Campo San Fantin 1965 | www.teatrolafenice.it | stop: Giglio*

TEATRO MALIBRAN
(122 C6) *(m K5–6)*

Opera, ballet, concerts and plays; some in cooperation with the Teatro Fenice. *Programme information and tickets tel. 04 12 42 24 | www.teatrolafenice.it | stop: Rialto*

WHERE TO STAY

Since Venice became one of the major magnets for international tourism many a generation ago, it has had a highly developed hotel business catering to all tastes.

The rich and famous will find palatial accommodation. Those looking for a middle-class hotel will have a hard time making up their mind. And even tourists with a limited budget will find a large choice of two and one-star hotels – although the simplest are often rather dark with tiny, minimally furnished rooms, where one of the guests may have to lie on the bed so that the other person can open the shower cubicle door.

Many of the rooms offered by the countless hotels and guesthouses in this labyrinthine city are really cramped and prices must quite clearly be described as being "above average". It is exceedingly difficult to find a half-way comfortable double room in a central location in the high season – and that runs from Easter to the end of October, as well as the period around Christmas, New Year and Carnival – for less than 140 euros, not to mention the fact that the municipality has instituted a so-called bed tax to help fill its perpetually empty coffers ranging from 1 to 5 euros per bed, per night (depending on hotel category, half this amount in off-peak season). Those who do not want to spend so much, should either reduce their expectations or come in winter when the spoiled hoteliers condescend to offering reduced rates. In any case, it is a good idea to book as long

Whether on the Canal Grande, in the midst of the labyrinth of small streets, or with a view of a beach on the Adriatic: the best places to stay

in advance as possible, especially for the high season. In spite of there being 400 hotels and guesthouses with around 24,000 beds in the Old town alone, there is often a shortage of accommodation – hardly surprising considering the almost 4 million overnight stays every year.

The *Venezia Si* organisation *(tel. 04 15 22 22 64 | www.veneziasi.it)* enables booking from home. If you call from Italy, the service number is *(*) 199 17 33 09*. A comfortable way to make a reservation is over the following internet websites: *www.*

booking.com, www.venicehotel.com and *www.cross-pollinate.com*. If Venice appears to be really sold out, you might still have some luck in one of the hotels near the railway station on Lista di Spagna or the Lido. Another alternative that is popular with families, even if they only stay for a few days, is to rent an apartment. These usually have separate areas for living and sleeping and a possibility to cook. Reduced prices are usual given for longer stays.

A word about prices: our classification – see page 4 – is based on the average price for the season in the most inexpensive double room in the hotel or guesthouse. As demand often exceeds supply, and there is hardly a genuine "off-season" in Venice, you should calculate on prices considerably above those quoted. On the other hand, the global economic crisis

On the Lido: the Hungaria Palace's striking majolica façade

has had a severe impact on Venice and an increasing number of hoteliers have been forced to lower their prices – a phenomenon that not only, but mainly, applies to the more expensive hotels which often grant substantial discounts now if the hotel is not fully booked. In any case, you should check the webiste of individual hotels and international sites for the latest special offers. And if you telephone to book when you arrive, always ask for

a *sconto* especially if you are staying for several nights.

HOTELS: EXPENSIVE

CONCORDIA ★ ✻
(126 C2–3) (*ⁿ K7*)

As central as it gets: the only hotel with a view of St Mark's Basilica and Square has a slightly chilly charm, but the service and comfort are first-rate. The breakfast buffet facing the Campanile is unforgettable. *56 rooms | Calle Larga San Marco 367 | tel. 04 15 20 68 66 | www.hotelconcordia.it | stop: San Marco*

HUNGARIA PALACE
(131 D–E3) (*ⁿ 0*)

A hotel gem lies hidden behind the fairy-tale art nouveau façade of majolica tiles on the main street on the Lido halfway between the lagoon and the Adriatic. Most of the furniture is still original art nouveau; there is an elegant dining room with a bar, a winter veranda and terrace. Authentic Thai spa *Lanna Gaia*. *88 rooms | Gran Viale Santa Maria Elisabetta 28 | tel. 04 12 42 00 60 | www.hotelhungaria. com | stop: Lido*

METROPOLE
(127 E3) (*ⁿ M8*)

Opulent, Baroque interior with gold-plated chandeliers, grandfather clocks and mirrors. The collection of corkscrews is another attraction. Excellent restaurant. Don't forget to ask for a room with a view of the lagoon! *67 rooms | Riva degli Schiavoni 4149 | tel. 04 15 20 50 44 | www.hotelmetropole.com | stop: San Zaccaria*

MONACO & GRAND CANAL ★ ●
(126 B–C4) (*ⁿ J8*)

Elegant, traditional hotel opposite Harry's Bar only a two-minute walk from Piazza

San Marco. Extremely chic furnishings and an exquisite, but expensive, restaurant (fantastic panorama from the ✿ terrace). Recently completely renovated and extended to include the neighbouring post-modern Palazzo Ridotto. *92 rooms | Calle Vallaresso 1332 | tel. 04 15 20 02 11 | www.hotelmonaco.it | stop: Vallaresso*

PALAZZINA GRASSI
(125 E3) (*ⓜ F7–8*)

The famous French designer Philippe Starck has turned this dainty building next to the museum of the same name into a gem of a contemporary hotel worthy of its five stars. With much attention to detail, the lobby, lounge, and restaurant/bar have been outfitted with a mix of vintage furniture and lush colours, but the 26 rooms have been kept all in white. *Ramo Grassi 3247 | tel. 04 15 28 46 44 | www.palazzinag.it | stop: San Samuele*

SATURNIA & INTERNATIONAL
(126 A4) (*ⓜ H8*)

A hotel palace from the 14th century. Most of the agreeably spacious rooms face the inner courtyard and ooze quality. *89 rooms | Calle Larga XXII Marzo 2398 | tel. 04 15 20 83 77 | www.hotelsaturnia.it | stop: Giglio*

HOTELS: MODERATE

ALA
(126 A4) (*ⓜ H8*)

Quality and modern comfort are the outstanding features in this two-winged house in the heart of San Marco. Suites under the roof and rooms with a jacuzzi are especially popular with romantic couples. *85 rooms | Campo Santa Maria del Giglio | tel. 04 15 20 83 33 | www.hotelala. it | stop: Giglio*

BECHER
(126 B3) (*ⓜ H8*)

A still rather new, very pleasant three-star hotel near Teatro Fenice. Breakfast in your room at no extra charge. Half of the rooms have a view of the canal. *17 rooms | Calle del Fruttarol 1857 | tel. 04 15 22 12 53 | www. hotelbecher.com | stop: Giglio*

BRIDGE
(127 D2) (*ⓜ L7*)

Small, perfectly furnished hotel behind St Mark's Basilica. *10 rooms | Calle Sacrestia 4498 | tel. 04 15 20 52 87 | www.hotelbridge. com | stop: San Zaccaria*

CASA REZZONICO
(125 D4) (*ⓜ E8*)

Informal hotel with antique furniture only two minutes from the trendy Campo Santa

---

MARCO POLO HIGHLIGHTS

⭐ **Concordia**
The perfect place to stay with a view of Saint Mark's Square
→ p. 84

⭐ **Monaco & Grand Canal**
Live in style in the centre of the city opposite Harry's Bar; enlarged with a post-modern Palazzo → p. 84

⭐ **Cipriani**
As good as its reputation
→ p. 86

⭐ **Danieli**
Luxury legend with a roof terrace and spectacular lobby
→ p. 86

⭐ **Generator Hostel Venice**
Youth hostel with a great view
→ p. 88

Margherita district. Breakfast is served in the tranquil little garden. *14 rooms | Fondamenta Gheradini 2813 | tel. 04 12 77 06 53 | www.casarezzonico.it | stop: Ca' Rezzonico*

GABRIELLI SANDWIRTH ✻
(127 F3) (*M N8*)

This Gothic-style building is full of atmosphere, has large rooms, an idyllic green courtyard and the view from the roof terrace is a dream. Don't forget to book a room looking towards the lagoon! *103 rooms | Riva degli Schiavoni 4110 | tel. 04 15 23 15 80 | www.hotelgabrieli.it | stop: Arsenale*

LOCANDA DEL GHETTO
(121 E3) (*M F2*)

Stay in the heart of the former Ghetto in a six-hundred-year-old building one floor below the former synagogue. Well looked-

LUXURY HOTELS

Cipriani ⭐ (131 D4) (*M K11*)

The Cipriani is located on the eastern tip of Giudecca surrounded by a luxuriant garden and with an outdoor pool. Connections day and night to the jetty at Saint Mark's Square in its own boats; perfect service. It is not surprising that this legendary hotel is considered one of Europe's top addresses. Rooms in the hotel's separate buildings, Palazzo Vendramin and Palazzetto Barbaro with views of Saint Mark's are even more magnificent. *95 rooms | double room from 980 euros | Giudecca 10 | tel. 0 41 24 08 01 | www.hotelcipriani.it*

Danieli ⭐ ⬤ ✻ (127 D3) (*M L8*)

The Doge's Palace and Saint Mark's Square are only a stone's throw away, the lagoon and San Giorgio Maggiore in front of the window. The hotel was originally owned by a doge's family and, with its silk wall coverings, Persian carpets and gold-plated mirrors, has been a home away from home for the rich and famous for generations. *225 rooms | double room from 360 euros | Riva degli Schiavoni 4196 | tel. 04 15 22 64 80 | www.danieli. hotelinvenice.com | stop: San Zaccaria*

Excelsior ✻ (131 D–E4) (*M O*)

This gigantic, Moorish-style complex erected on the sandy beach at the Lido in 1907 stands out from far away. The atmosphere in this luxurious hotel with its spacious restaurants is one of *grandezza*, especially during the Film Festival. *197 rooms and suites | double room from 330 euros | Lungomare Marconi 41 | tel. 04 15 26 02 01 | excelsior.hotelinvenice.com | stop: Lido*

The St Regis Venice
San Clemente Palace ⬤ (127 D4)

The incredible sum of 100 million euros was necessary to transform this former monastery, whose origins go back almost 900 years, only 10 minutes by motorboat from Saint Mark's Square, into a super-luxury hotel, with valuable antiques and the greatest comfort imaginable. There are three gourmet restaurants, a large spa, an open-air pool, several tennis courts and even a small golf course. *191 rooms and suites | double room from 570 euros | tel. 04 14 75 01 11 | www. stregisvenice.com | private shuttle boat from San Marco*

after, good breakfast, pleasant service. The two junior suites have INSIDER TIP charming terraces overlooking the central square. *6 rooms | Campo del Ghetto Novo 2892 | tel. 04 12 75 92 92 | www.locan dadelgheto.net | stop: Guglie*

INSIDER TIP AL PONTE MOCENIGO
(121 F5) (*m* G4)

Tastefully styled standard hotel, pleasantly low-priced. Breakfast and drinks in the shady courtyard. All rooms with bathroom and air-conditioning. *10 rooms | Fondamenta Rimpetto Mocenigo 2063 | tel. 04 15 24 47 97 | www.alpontemocenigo. com | stop: San Stae*

SAN GALLO
(126 B3) (*m* J7)

Small, charming hotel on a *campo* that is just as lovely only a few yards north of Piazza San Marco with a breakfast terrace on the roof. *12 rooms | Campo San Gallo 1093a | tel. 04 15 22 73 11 | www.hotelsan gallo.com | stops: Rialto, Vallaresso*

VILLA MABAPA ☼
(131 E4) (*m* 0)

Airy, smart hotel in a villa at the northern corner of the Lido that is hardly affected by tourism. Lovely view of the old city, restaurant with garden terrace. *66 rooms | Riviera San Nicolò 16 | tel. 04 15 26 05 90 | www.villamabapa.com | stop: Lido*

HOTELS: BUDGET

INSIDER TIP ANGELIKA
(131 E4) (*m* 0)

A bit away from the hustle and bustle of the Lido but still only a five-minute walk from the *vaporetto*: two tasteful, reasonably priced B&B rooms and a flat for families. Helpful owner; bicycles available. *Via Antonio Loredan 12a | c/o Fehle*

Franco | tel. 04 15 26 87 01 | www.angelika lido.com | stop: Lido

CA' DEL DOSE
(127 F3) (*m* M8)

Charming guesthouse in a side street at the eastern end of Riva degli Schiavoni. Modern atmosphere in warm colours, functionally furnished, air-conditioning, friendly service. *6 rooms | Calle del Dose 3801 | tel. 04 15 20 98 87 | www.cadeldose. com | stop: Arsenale*

CAPRERA
(121 D4) (*m* E4)

If you can do without an en-suite bathroom, this is a cheap place to stay near the railway station. Some of the renovated rooms have a small balcony – it's worth asking for one! *14 rooms | Lista di Spagna 219 | tel. 0 41 71 52 71 | www.hotel caprera.it | stop: Ferrovia*

INSIDER TIP CERTOSA
(131 D–E 3–4) (*m* 0)

This place is not only an alternative to normal hotels in the Old City for water sports' enthusiasts: the small, very personally-run hotel is attached to the extremely modern yachting centre that has been established on the island of the same name. Smart, functional, decorated in cheerful colours and with spacious gardens, but only a few minutes by *vaporetto* from the *centro storico*, it is a real oasis of tranquillity. ⚫ You can rent canoes and boats to explore the lagoon at your own pace. *25 rooms | Certosa Island | tel. 04 12 77 86 32 | www.ventodi venezia.com | stop: Certosa*

DONI
(127 D–E3) (*m* L7–8)

This pleasant guesthouse with wooden floors is a place where you will feel at home. The only drawback: nine of the 13 rooms have their bathroom on the landing. *Calle del Vin 4656 | tel. 04 15 22 42 67 | www.albergodoni.it | stop: San Zaccaria*

AI DUE FANALI
(121 D5) (*∅ E4*)

Quiet, impeccable hotel, with reasonable prices, only a few yards from the railway station. An interesting alternative for groups: the owner also has four suites, each of 50m^2 and with three beds on the Riva degli Schiavoni. Main building: *16 rooms | Campo San Simeon Grande 946 | tel. 04 17 18 84 90 | www.aiduefanali.com | stop: Ferrovia*

LOW BUDGET

The youth hostel with what is probably the most beautiful view in the world is located on the northern side of Giudecca with a panorama of the Doge's Palace and Campanile. It is open all year round and reservations are essential. An overnight stay in a dorm with breakfast costs 16–60 euros, depending on the season. ★ ⚓ *Generator Hostel Venice* **(131 D4)** (*∅ J11*) *(27 rooms with 235 beds | | Fondamenta delle Zitelle 86 | tel. 04 18 77 82 88 | www.generatorhostels.com | stop: Zitelle*

Another alternative to the hotels in Venice is the *Campeggio San Nicolò* **(131 E4)** (*∅ 0*) *(Via di Sammicheli 14 | tel. 04 15 26 74 15 | www.camping-sannicolo.com)*: this is a well-run camp site with space for 174 tents on the north tip of the Lido. And there are plenty of other reasonably-priced camp sites on the mainland to the north of Venice. *www.assocamping.it*

GUERRATO
(122 B6) (*∅ J5*)

This small, simple, but well cared-for *albergo* is located in an 800-year-old building and has, by Venetian standards, comparatively large, bright rooms, some of them with a picturesque view of the vegetable market. *20 rooms | Calle dietro la Scimmia 240a | tel. 04 15 28 59 27 | www.pensioneguerrato.it | stop: Rialto*

PAGANELLI (127 E3) (*∅ L8*)

Breathtaking views of the lagoon from the ⚓ rooms on the south side of this hotel. The other building on nearby Campo San Zaccaria is just as good. *22 rooms | Riva degli Schiavoni 4687 | tel. 04 15 22 43 24 | www.hotelpaganelli.com | stop: San Zaccaria*

INSIDER TIP ▸ SANT'ANNA
(129 D4) (*∅ Q8*)

Well-maintained, very pleasant one-star accommodation in a quiet location at the edge of the old city centre just a three minutes' walk from the Biennale grounds. Terrace solarium, relaxed atmosphere, rooms with bath (from 50 euros) and without (from 45 euros). *8 rooms | Corte del Bianco 269 | tel. 04 15 28 64 66 | www.locandasantanna.com | stop: Giardini*

PENSIONE SEGUSO ⚓
(125 E6) (*∅ F10*)

The atmosphere in this wonderfully old-fashioned guesthouse is perfect for sentimental souls. The rooms have views of Giudecca or a picturesque side canal. Half-board is obligatory in the high season. Advance booking recommended! *36 rooms | Zattere ai Gesuati 779 | tel. 04 15 28 68 58 | www.pensionesegusovenice.com | stop: Zattere*

Stylish youth hostel with a fabulous, panoramic view

LOCANDA SILVA (127 D2) (𝄞 K7)
Bright and friendly double rooms from 85 euros plus nice staff, located just a two-minute walk to the northeast of San Marco on a picturesque canal. *23 rooms | Fondamenta del Rimedio 4423 | tel. 04 15 22 76 43 | www.locandasilva.it | stop: San Zaccaria*

INSIDER TIP OSTELLO VENISSA ⓥ
(131 E3) (𝄞 V1)
A taste of rural Venice for connoisseurs on the little island of Mazzorbo next to Burano. This country estate with extensive gardens features an organic gourmet restaurant as well as a small hotel in the main house with 6 airy and charming rooms decorated with a mix of contemporary and country-style furnishings. Double rooms from 100 euros. *Fondamenta Santa Caterina 3 | tel. 04 15 27 22 81 | www. venissa.it | stop: Mazzorbo*

FLATS

Venice's high-price hotels have led to holiday flats becoming increasingly popular with its guests. The following enterprises can provide a large number of good addresses, especially ones that are not so expensive (sometimes, also guesthouses offering B&B): *www.welcomevenice.com (tel. 04 15 22 52 51), www.appartamentivenezia.it (tel. 33 46 04 58 50), www. veniceapartment.com, www.viewsonvenice.com (tel. 04 12 411149) and www. cabadoer-veniceflat.it.*

INSIDER TIP ALLOGGI TEMPORANEI
(125 E4) (𝄞 G8)
This agency has around 100 different places to stay, ranging from single rooms in private homes to spacious flats. *Calle Vitturi o Faller 2923 | tel. 04 15 23 16 72 | www.mwz-online.com | stop: San Samuele*

CA' DELLA CORTE
The people who run this average-standard hotel ((124 C2) (𝄞 E6) Corte Surian 3560) also have four elegant flats to rent. Very comfortable and fully equipped, suitable for families with small children, luggage transfer, laundry service – and even breakfast can be provided. *Tel. 0 41 71 58 77 | www.cadellacorte.com | stop: Piazzale Roma*

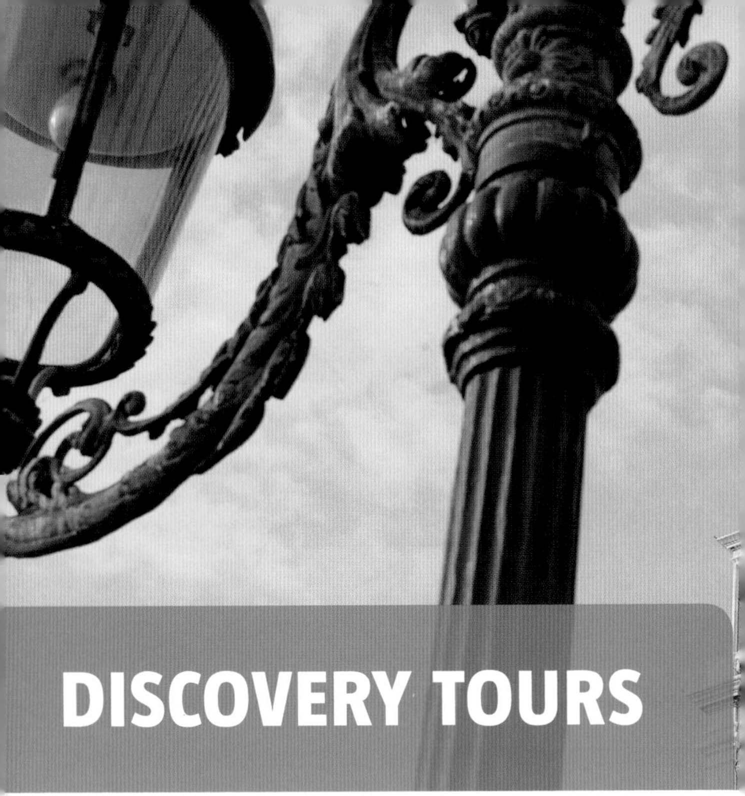

DISCOVERY TOURS

1 VENICE AT A GLANCE

START: 1 Santa Lucia train station
END: 15 Art Blu Caffè

Distance:
approx. 12 km/7.5 miles

1 day
Walking time (without stops) approx. 3 ½ hours

COSTS: 100–150 euros/person (day ticket for local transportation, admission fees, food, coffee, drinks, evening concert tickets)
WHAT TO PACK: rain gear or sun protection as needed

IMPORTANT TIPS: you can vary the starting point of this tour depending on the location of your hotel – just start from the closest *vaporetti* stop to your neighbourhood.
You can only tour the Cathedral and climb the Campanile at the times provided during the main season between Easter and October because these attractions close earlier at other times of the year.
You should try to purchase concert tickets well in advance of your trip.

 Photo: Campanile di San Marco

Cities have many faces. If you want to get behind the scenes to explore their unique charm and head off the beaten track or find your way to green oases, handpicked restaurants or the best local activities, then these tailored Discovery Tours are just the right thing. Choose the best route for the day and follow in the footsteps of the MARCO POLO authors – well-prepared to navigate your way to all the many highlights that await you along the tour.

Get to know Venice at its best in just one eventful day with this tour packed full of the city's highlights.

08:00am At the **①** Santa Lucia train station, take a **Line 1** *vaporetto* **to San Silvestro.** In the morning light, the glistening façades of the palaces along the Canal Grande breeze past – there really is no better way to begin a day exploring the grandeur of this city on the lagoon! Stop for a coffee near Rialto bridge at **②** Caffè del Doge → p. 64. **Then head northwards and go around two or three cor-**

① Santa Lucia train station

② Caffè del Doge

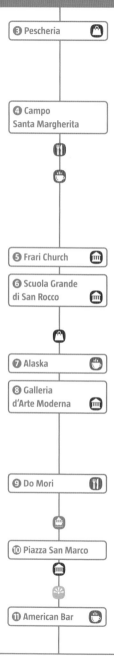

❸ Pescheria

❹ Campo Santa Margherita

❺ Frari Church

❻ Scuola Grande di San Rocco

❼ Alaska

❽ Galleria d'Arte Moderna

❾ Do Mori

❿ Piazza San Marco

⓫ American Bar

ners to get to the ❸ **Pescheria** → p. 31. Stroll past the fishmongers' stalls *(Tue–Sat)* and enjoy this amazing feast for the eyes even if you don't plan on buying anything!

09:30am Now it's time for a good breakfast. There is hardly a better place to soak up the atmosphere of the city than ❹ **Campo Santa Margherita** → p. 52, which is just a ten minutes' walk away. **Go past Campo San Polo and the Frari Church** and then sit down at one of the tables at **Caffè Rosso** → p. 80 **on the western side.** It's a great place to observe the goings-on of daily life in Venice away from the tourist crowds.

10:30am Sufficiently replenished, you're ready to tackle one of the day's first highlights **just a few minutes to the north on foot**, namely the pyramid-shaped tomb of Titian and his painting of the Ascension above the main altar of the ❺ **Frari Church** → p. 49. **Right next door** to this magnificent church is the ❻ **Scuola Grande di San Rocco** → p. 52. Make sure to take a good look at is main hall adorned with 56 paintings by Jacopo Tintoretto.

12:30pm Afterwards, walk through the **alleyways of San Polo** with its souvenir and craftsmen's shops. **Take a little detour to Santa Croce** and check out Carlo Pistacchi's Gelateria ❼ **Alaska** → p. 64. Your next destination is the one of the most impressive palaces **on the Canal Grande**, which now houses the ❽ **Galleria d'Arte Moderna** → p. 30. The collection in Ca' Pesaro → p. 30 contains a representative selection of 19th and 20th century art.

02:30pm A number of quaint, old wine taverns **around the Rialto bridge** have survived the various waves of modernisation intact. The oldest of these so-called *bacari* is the picture-perfect ❾ **Do Mori** → p. 63. Enjoy fabulous wine and delicious *cicheti* at the bar!

03:30pm The Line 1 *vaporetto* (stop: Rialto Mercato) will **bring you directly to the** ❿ **Piazza San Marco** → p. 40 in a matter of minutes. After visiting the **cathedral** and taking the lift up to the top of the **Campanile**, stop for coffee or a refreshing drink and let the scenery work its magic around you. Your options here include some of the famous fancy cafés such as Florian → p. 65 or Quadri → p. 65, but a much more affordable choice (with plenty of bread rolls) is the ⓫ **American Bar** → p. 62 **at the foot of the clock tower** with its standing tables.

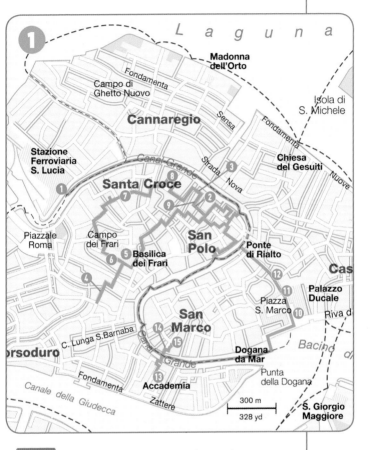

05:00pm A bit of shopping is up next on the agenda. **Stroll through the ⑫ Mercerie → p. 70 towards the Rialto bridge**. Almost all the major fashion designers have boutiques along the narrow streets, which are also dotted with enticing shops selling exquisite jewellery and antiques. **At the Rialto pier, hop aboard a Line 1 *vaporetto* and get off at Accademia.**

07:00pm **Follow along the eastern flank of the famous gallery of paintings** until you come to the Hotel Ca' Pisani. You might be tempted to stay longer than you originally planned in its basement wine bar ⑬ La Rivista → p. 63 that serves snacks and wines by the glass.

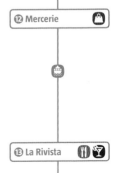

⑫ Mercerie

⑬ La Rivista

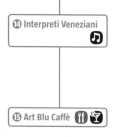

⑭ Interpreti Veneziani ♫

08:00pm But, you don't really want to let your tickets for a concert at the ⑭ **Interpreti Veneziani** → p. 78 go to waste. Experience Baroque chamber music at its finest surrounded by the suggestive ambiance of a former church! **Afterwards, cross the Ponte dell'Accademia to get to San Vidal in less than five minutes.**

⑮ Art Blu Caffè 🍴 🍸

10:00pm Are you ready for a late supper? **Right around the corner,** at the ⑮ **Art Blu Caffè** → p. 79, you can enjoy delicious food and good drinks whilst appreciating the view of Campo Santo Stefano at night.

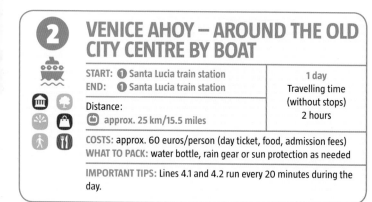

② VENICE AHOY – AROUND THE OLD CITY CENTRE BY BOAT

START: ❶ Santa Lucia train station END: ❶ Santa Lucia train station	1 day Travelling time (without stops) 2 hours
Distance: 🚌 approx. 25 km/15.5 miles	

COSTS: approx. 60 euros/person (day ticket, food, admission fees)
WHAT TO PACK: water bottle, rain gear or sun protection as needed

IMPORTANT TIPS: Lines 4.1 and 4.2 run every 20 minutes during the day.

The best way to explore the historic heart of the city of canals is on the water. Instead of embarking on the classic route along the main artery, the Canal Grande, try a tour around the city for a change. Aboard a Line 4.1 or 4.2 *vaporetto,* you will become acquainted with the lesser-known Cannaregio district and the harbour area as well as Murano and the cemetery island as you enjoy panoramic views of Venice's most beautiful waterside promenades.

❶ Santa Lucia train station

The starting point for this tour is the ❶ Santa Lucia train station. At the bottom of the steps, board one of the floating buses so characteristic of the city of canals called a *vaporetto,* **serving Line 4.2** (Line 4.1 travels the same route, but in the opposite direction). At first, the boat chugs briefly along the Canal Grande. But, immediately after passing the impressive church of San Geremia – it turns left onto the Canale di Cannaregio. Leaving the Palazzo Labia behind, the route continues into the unusually spacious and bright district - at least according Venetian standards - of Cannaregio. **You should interrupt your journey at the first**

A master of glass blowing at work on Murano

stop (Ponte delle Guglie) and walk to the former Jewish ➋ Ghetto → p. 47, which is also the world's oldest. You can learn more about its history in the museum.

Back on board the *vaporetto,* you will float under the triple-arched Ponte dei Tre Archi out onto the open water. The view stretches as far as Burano, Torcello and the airport as the boat steers to the east. Disembark briefly at the stop Madonna dell'Orto to see the wonderfully beautiful Gothic church of ➌ Madonna dell'Orto → p. 48 and the nearby ➍ last residence of Jacopo Tintoretto. You should get off again at the next stop, Fondamente Nove, and explore the Baroque Jesuit Church of ➎ Santa Maria Assunta dei Gesuiti → p. 47 and ➏ Titian's Residence.

Now head back onto the boat to glide on to ➐ San Michele → p. 57. By no means should you miss out on a walk across this cemetery island with its quite special atmosphere and famous graves, such as those of Igor Stravinsky and Sergei Diaghilev! The northernmost point along this round-trip route is the island of ➑ Murano → p. 58, famous for its traditional glass blowing industry. Art lovers should definitely take a look inside the churches of San Pietro Martire and Santi Maria e Donato. Sou-

➋ Ghetto

➌ Madonna dell'Orto

➍ last residence of Jacopo Tintoretto

➎ Santa Maria Assunta dei Gesuiti

➏ Titian's Residence

➐ San Michele

➑ Murano

venir shoppers, on the other hand, should make their way to one of the glassblowers' workshops open to visitors.

Return to the Fondamente Nove stop and take the *vaporetto* along the northern shore of the Castello district. It passes the Franciscan church called San Francesco della Vigna and navigates around the San Pietro di Castello and Isola di Sant'Elena peninsulas. Once it reaches the San Marco basin, it steers past the Biennale exhibition grounds to the west. As you pass by ⑨ **Riva degli Schiavoni**, the Dalmatians' Quay that is a popular place to go for a stroll because it is so broad, you can enjoy INSIDER TIP the parade of some of the most famous hotels in the city.

Is your stomach grumbling? Then **get off the boat one last time at San Zaccaria. Just 200 m (218 yd) away via Calle degli Albanesi awaits** ⑩ **Aciugheta** → p. 62 with its tasty snacks. **Once you are back on the boat,** you will drift past the island of Giudecca before **coming to the ferry harbour and crossing under the controversial Ponte della Costituzione → p. 30 to return to** ① **Santa Lucia train station.**

⑨ Riva degli Schiavoni

⑩ Aciugheta

① Santa Lucia train station

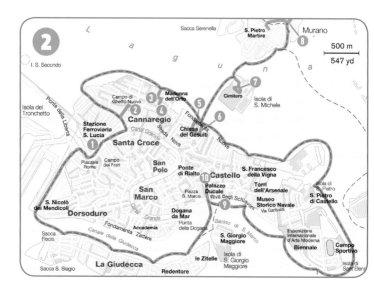

3 IN THE FOOTSTEPS OF PALLADIO

START: ❶ San Marco-San Zaccaria stop
END: ❼ Skyline Rooftop Bar

3–4 hours
Walking time
(without stops)
approx. 45 minutes

Distance:
🡆 3 km/1.8 miles on foot

COSTS: approx. 60 euros/person (day ticket for local transportation, food, coffee, drinks, admission fees incl. monastery tour)
WHAT TO PACK: rain gear or sun protection as needed

This walking tour leads you to the magnificent sacral buildings designed by the master architect Andrea Palladio from Padua. You will also get to know to the two islands to the south of the old city centre, San Giorgio Maggiore and Giudecca.

Take a Line 2 *vaporetto* **from the** ❶ **San Marco-San Zaccaria stop to cross over to San Giorgio Maggiore in a matter of minutes.** As you do so, you can take in the most popular photo motif in this city on the lagoon, namely the monastery of ❷ **San Giorgio Maggiore.** It was built at the end of the 16th century for the Benedictines by Andrea Palladio on the picturesque island across from the Doge's Palace. **Once you have reached the church itself,** take a moment to fully appreciate the geometrical austerity of its dazzling white marble façade reminiscent of an ancient temple before you take a look at the equally impressive interior of this three-nave church with its large Tintoretto paintings.

The panoramic view from the top of the **Campanile di San Giorgio Maggiore** *(daily 9:30am–12:30pm and 2:30pm–6pm, in winter only until 4:30pm)* is just as breathtaking as the view from the Campanile of San Marco across the way.

In order to admire another one of Palladio's masterpieces, all you have to do is **travel two stops on the same** *vaporetto* **line as before.** The votive church ❸ **Il Redentore** *(Mon–Sat 10am–5pm)* will rise up before you on the neighbouring island of Giudecca. This classicist-style dome church with its impressive marble façade was designed by Palladio for the city government as an offering to thank God for ending the plague epidemic in the city. It was consecrated in 1592 and it has been the focal point of a large annual festival held on the third Sunday in July in which

❶ San Marco-
San Zaccaria stop

❷ San Giorgio
Maggiore

❸ Il Redentore

the Venetians commemorate the deliverance of the city from the plague ever since.

4 Santa Maria della Presentazione

The design of the church **4 Santa Maria della Presentazione** *(open only in summer Fri/Sat 3:30pm–6:30pm | as a precaution, call ahead tel. 04 15 32 29 20)*, which towers above the north quay of Giudecca **just a few minutes' walk to the east**, is also attributed to Andrea Palladio, although this is probably a mistake. Thanks to its majestic simplicity, this little church, whose nickname is Le Zitelle, is definitely worth a visit.

By now it's time to give your mind and body a rest. **Take a *vaporetto* two stops to the west. Directly behind the stop bearing the same name**, the trattoria **5 La Palanca** *(Mon–Sat noon–2:30pm, Bar 7am–8:30pm | tel. 04 15 28 77 19 | Budget)* offers lunch dishes or snacks as well as a fantastic view of the Zatterre from the tables along the water. Once you have had your fill, take a little detour towards the middle of the island. **Go through the Calle del Forno, then head left on Campo Junghans and follow along Rio del Ponte Lungo until you reach the open water. About 700 m (765 yd) further west**, you should definitely take a look at the **6 showroom** *(Mon–Fri 10am–1pm and 2pm–6pm | Fondamenta San Biagio 805)* of Fortuny, the legendary creator of luxury textiles – they are a feast for the eyes!

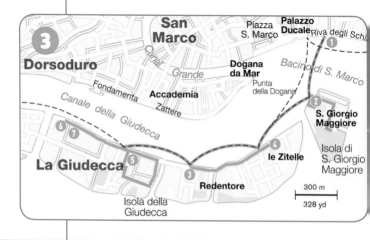

Andrea Palladio's masterpiece: San Giorgio Maggiore on the monastery island

The perfect way to end the day, **right nearby on the other side of the small canal**, is INSIDER TIP▸ to go up to the roof of the Molino Stucky Hilton Hotel. Enjoy a pleasant drink in the ❼ **Skyline Rooftop Bar** *(daily, in winter Tue–Sun 5pm–1am)* as you admire the magical view of the city and its lagoon.

❼ Skyline Rooftop Bar

❹ EXPLORING THE LESSER-KNOWN ISLANDS IN THE LAGOON

START: ❶ Fondamente Nove stop END: ❻ Lazzaretto Nuovo	1/2 day Time on board 1 hour, walking time approx. 2 hours
Distance: ➡ approx. 10 km/6.2 miles	

COSTS: approx. 50 euros/person (day ticket local transporation, food), 7 euros for a tour inside ❻ Lazzaretto Nuovo (optional).

WHAT TO PACK: sturdier shoes for cross-country walks, rain gear or sun protection as needed

IMPORTANT TIPS: tours of ❻ Lazzaretto Nuovo only offered Sat/Sun

The three islands of Murano, Burano and Torcello are well-known destinations for excursions, but the many smaller islands in the north of the lagoon are also worth a trip. They will show you the more rural side of Venice where you can walk through the trees and learn about local nature.

The best place to begin your tour is Venice's "vegetable island". It takes just 15 minutes by boat to get from the ❶ **Fondamente Nove stop** to the island of ❷ **Le Vignole**. **Walk along the main path from the jetty to the little bridge and cross over the main canal. Follow the right-hand path** through the vegetable fields to ❸ **Trattoria alle Vignole** *(closed Mon and Oct–Mar | tel. 04 15 28 97 07 | Budget)*. It's a good bet that the fish and meat dishes served on the simple wooden tables outside will taste particularly good alongside the view of Venice's silhouette! Only private boats with special authorization are permitted to access the famous maritime fortress of Sant'Andrea on the southern tip of the island. Constructed by the famous master builder Michele Sanmicheli in the 16th century, its canons once kept the enemies of the La Serenissima from approaching the city by sea.

The island of ❹ **Sant'Erasmo** further to the north is even more peaceful. It is the second, but much larger garden before the doors of Venice. **Take a Line 13 *vaporetto* from Le Vignole to get to the island's stop Capannone. Walk about 15 minutes to the south** to the ❺ **Torre Massimiliana** *(April–Oct Wed–Fri 2pm–6pm, Sat/Sun 10am–6pm)*, a

❶ Fondamente Nove stop

❷ Le Vignole

❸ Trattoria alle Vignole

❹ Sant'Erasmo

❺ Torre Massimiliana

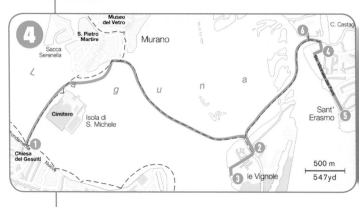

The patchwork quilt of idyllic green islands in the north of the lagoon

fortified brick tower dating back to the Austrian occupation that now hosts interesting contemporary art exhibitions.

The little island of ⑥ Lazzaretto Nuovo lies across from the aforementioned Stazione Capannone. Thanks to its strategic location, it has been used by the Venetians and different occupiers as a military base at different points in history. From the 15th to the 18th centuries, it also protected La Serenissima against epidemics as it served as a quarantine station for people and goods. For some years now, archaeologists and ecologists have been devoting more attention to this long neglected and almost forgotten island.

As part of an "island revival" campaign, a team of local volunteers now offers highly recommendable INSIDER TIP nature and history walks from April to October at the weekend *(Sat/Sun 9:45am and 4:30pm | tel. 04 12 44 40 11 | www.lazzarettonuovo.com)*. If you wish to take part in one of these tours, then you need to **board a *vaporetto* in Sant'Erasmo heading for Lazzaretto Nuovo around 4:15pm**. During the tour, you will learn more about Venice during the plague and you will get to see some of the defensive walls and huge warehouses – in particular the so-called Teson Grande filled with museum objects – as well as a documentary film. On the half-hour nature walk along the island's outer walls, informative display boards describe the flora and fauna found in the lagoon area.

⑥ Lazzaretto Nuovo

TRAVEL WITH KIDS

In Venice you will look in vain for the classical "highlights for kids in cities" such as a museum or theatre just for them, or a zoo and special tours. But Venice's completely different lifestyle will more than compensate for that.

As a rule, climbing one of the towers and admiring the view from the top is a hit. And, they can have a lot of fun playing football or hide-and-seek with the local kids in one of the many playgrounds such as those on the *campi San Polo*, *Santa Margherita* and *Giacomo dell'Orto*. An absolute must either before or while visiting Venice is to read Cornelia Funke's *The Thief Lord* that takes young readers on a wonderfully exciting trip to the mysterious "floating city" and will make them look forward to it even more. It has been successfully filmed and also adapted for the theatre.

LAGOON ADVENTURE ⚓
(131 D–E 2–5) *(∅ 0)*
In addition to the small islands that can be reached by *vaporetto* (see chapter "Discovery Tours") many other treasures in the areas of natural and art history are waiting to be discovered in the lagoon: archaeological sights, historical fortresses, saltworks, bird reserves and traditional fishermen's huts that are still in use today. The *Operatori Naturalisti Limosa (tel. 0 41 93 20 03 | www.limosa. it, www.slowvenice.it, www.natura-venezia.it)* and *Sestante di Venezia (tel. 04 12 41 39 87 | www.sestantedivenezia. it)* organise INSIDER TIP tours that will also fascinate children. A very special way to really get a feel for the charm of the more distant canals and islets is on board a *bragozzo*, an old-fashioned wooden freight barge. A number of excellent organisers are listed at *www. guidetovenice.it* (heading: The Lagoon); you can also call 32 89 48 56 71 for more info in English.

LIDO ●
(131 D–E4) *(∅ 0)*
A (half)day on the Lido swimming and building sand castles makes a welcome change. There is a playground next to the Planetarium on *Lungomare D'Annunzio*. Another contrast programme could be a bike outing to the south-west of the Lido, which is surprisingly green in some parts. There are two places *(noleggio cicli)* where you can hire bicycles, tandems and rickshaws for four at the Lido *vaporetto* stop: *Gardin (Piazza Santa Maria*

Off to the Lido! Canals, the lagoon and the beach island: a change of pace for kids tired of culture and museums

Elisabetta 2 | tel. 04 12 76 00 05 | www. biciclettegardin.com) and *Renato Scarpi (Viale Santa Maria Elisabetta 21b | tel. 04 15 26 80 19 | www.lidoonbike.it).*

PALAZZO DUCALE SPECIALE
(127 D3) *(ᗉ K8)*

Along "secret routes" *(itinerari segreti)* through the Doge's Palace: an adventure for youngsters, even if they don't understand a word. The tours are held every morning – twice in Italian, French and English – and take you along narrow corridors to the most distant corners of the palace including the false ceiling of the Great Council Hall, and to the dark dungeon where Giacomo Casanova once spent some time. Bookings at the information counter at the entrance to the palace or, at least 48 hours in advance, from abroad by *tel. 0 41 42 73 08 92* as well as online under *www.palazzoducale.visitmuve.it*

ROWING, ALLA VENEZIANA

Two tome-honoured rowing clubs give short courses lasting only a few days to teach beginners and children (from around ten to twelve) how to manoeuvre a *sandolo, mascareta* or *gondola* elegantly over the water and through the canals. *Società Canottieri Bucintoro* (126 A6) *(ᗉ H10) (Zattere 261 | tel. 04 15 20 56 30 | www.bucintoro.org | 5 hours, 55 euros; 10 hours, 100 euros)* and *Canottieri F. Querini (123 E5) (ᗉ M5) (Fondamente Nove 6576e | tel. 04 15 22 20 39 | www. canottieriquerini.it | 8 lessons, 100 euros).*

THROUGH THE CANALS BY BOAT
(121 D4) *(ᗉ F3)*

Exploring the labyrinth of canals on your own in a rented boat is a very special kind of adventure. The best address for renting rowing boats or motorised vessels is *Giampetro Brussa (Calle Fondamenta Labia 331 | tel. 0 41 71 57 87 | www.brussaisboat.it)* next to Ponte delle Guglie.

FESTIVALS & EVENTS

JANUARY/FEBRUARY

Capodanno in Spiaggia (New Year at the Beach): All night-owls on the Lido are given snacks and warm drinks at sunrise

6 Jan: Befana the "good" witch makes an appearance at the **Children's Festivities at Sant'Erasmo**

Mid-Jan to Shrove Tueday: the legendary ★ ● **Carnevale** with improvised performances, balls and a sea of masks on squares and streets. *www.carnevale.venezia.it*

Ash Wednesday: end of Carnival with the symbolic INSIDER**TIP** **Cremation of Pantalone** on a funeral pyre, followed by a **masked procession** on the Riva degli Schiavoni

MARCH/APRIL

On a Sunday in March: ***Su e Zo per i Ponti*** – running race "up and down the bridges". *www.suezo.it*

Maundy Thursday: **Benedizione del Fuoco** – when St Mark's Basilica glows in the light of thousands of candles.

25 April: **Festa di San Marco** with a solemn mass in the Basilica, gondola races on the Canal Grande and festivities on the Piazza

MAY/JUNE

1 May: ● ***Sagra dea Sparesea*** – "Asparagus Festival" in Cavallino with an open race and regatta, celebrations and fireworks

On a Sunday in May: ***Vogalonga*** – the great open regatta from San Marco across the lagoon (see p. 44)

Sunday after Ascension: **Festa della Sensa** – "Marriage with the Sea" with a historical fleet sailing from San Marco to the Lido

MID-JUNE TO EARLY NOVEMBER

★ ***Venice Art Biennale*** in odd years in the exhibition area in the eastern section of the Castello district: painters, sculptors, installation and video artists get together for the **Esposizione Internazionale d'Art**. Also worth visiting to see the architecture of some of the pavilions created by stars such as Alvar Aalto, Josef Hoffmann and the Aldrich & Delanor team. *www.labiennale.org*

JULY

Second Sunday: ● ***Fishermen's Festival at Malamocco*** with regatta and fish feast

Third Sunday: ***Redentore*** "Feast of the Saviour" with beautiful procession to the Redentore church; amazing display

Not only Carnival: Venice's calendar of festivities has something for everyone – from the exuberant to the more contemplative

of INSIDER TIP *fireworks* on the night before

SEPTEMBER
First weekend: *Regata Storica* – thousands of festively decorated boats with historically-costumed crews glide down the Canal Grande
International Film Festival on the Lido. *www.labiennale.org*
Third Sunday: *Fish Festival* on Burano

END OF SEPTEMBER/EARLY OCTOBER
INSIDER TIP *Festival dell'Aria:* a weekend for all fans of air sports: an air show that takes place alternately on the airports of Nicelli at the Lido and Allegri in Padua. *www.festivaldellaria.it*

OCTOBER
First Sunday: ● *Wine Festival* on Sant' Erasmo with music, dancing, feasting and a regatta
Late October: *Venice Marathon* starting in Stra. *www.venicemarathon.it*

NOVEMBER
21 Nov: *Madonna della Salute* – procession over pontoons to the church followed by a feast with raisin donuts and wine

NATIONAL HOLIDAYS

1 Jan	*Capodanno*
6 Jan	*Epifania*
March/April	*Pasquetta* (Easter Monday)
25 April	*Liberazione* (Day of liberation from fascism)
1 May	*Festa del Lavoro*
2 June	*Giorno della Repubblica* (Day of the Republic)
15 Aug	*Ferragosto*
1 Nov	*Ognissanti*
8 Dec	*Immacolata Concezione* (Immaculate Conception)
25 Dec	*Natale*
26 Dec	*Santo Stefano*

LINKS, BLOGS, APPS & MORE

LINKS & BLOGS

maps.veniceconnected.it Here you will find an interactive city map. Click on the sights and make a virtual tour of the squares and streets – fantastic! An exciting way to get a first overview

www.panoramio.com An international photo-sharing website with an extensive archive of artistic photographs as beautiful as paintings. Enter "Venice Italy" in the search field for a wide selection of beautiful photographs of the city from various perspectives and revel in its atmosphere

www.timeout.com/venice Up-to-date, hand-picked descriptions of major attractions, hotels, restaurants, bars and shops

www.veniceonline.it an excellent resource for everything you want to know about being a tourist in Venice. It has the entire city's transport information as well as maps, photos, videos, audio guides, cultural events, restaurants, webcams and much more

www.europeforvisitors.com/venice Private travel-planning site for Venice with lots of useful advice, including information for cruise ship tourists and sections like "The top 11 Mistakes"

www.venetiancat.blogspot.com is the popular blog by author and newspaper contributor Cat Bauer who has lived on the Canal Grande in Venice for a number of years. The blog has been featured in a number of international publications and is an insider's view of the expat life in Venice

venicewiki.org Even if you don't speak Italian, this Wiki will provide you much valuable and useful information ranging from Venetian songs to a dialect dictionary

www.ogvenice.com/blog Tasteful private travel guide with blog and detailed texts about topics like Murano glass, bookstores or Venetian aperitifs

thevenice experience.blog-spot.com Two American expats write about everyday life in Venice

Regardless of whether you are still preparing your trip or already in Venice: these addresses will provide you with more information, videos and networks to make your holiday even more enjoyable.

www.youtube.com/watch?v=4K_mvsDSUi4 Trailer for an art DVD with examples of 3D tours through Canaletto paintings, bringing Canaletto's Venice back to life

vimeo.com/73552615 In five minutes, 13 beautiful spots on and around Venice's canals are captured – in slow motion and accompanied by the "Chorus of the Hebrew Slaves" from Verdi's *Nabucco*

https://www.youtube.com/watch?v=UN-II_jBzzo A history lesson with a difference: The relationship between Venice and the Ottoman Empire explained with quirky animations

www.learnitalianpod.com A free online resource that teaches Italian grammar, pronunciation and practical Italian phrases for use in everyday situations through the means of downloadable podcasts

Venice Giracittà is an English-language audio guide has more than four hours of information on the city: from busy squares to narrow lanes to mysterious places

Worldview iPhone App shows you where all of Venice's webcams are. Simply click and decide if it is worth making a detour

Venice 2Go is an offline map and city guide with a wide selection of articles, points of interest and landmarks with a focuses on the city's history

The Essential Green Travel Guide Eco-conscious Venice travellers in particular will love this iPhone App: It shows everything a hip Loha person needs – from weekly markets selling organic produce, slow food restaurants and fair trade products to yoga studios

mTrip Guide The ultimate Venice App for iPhone and Android not only has the typical travel guide information on offer, but also many tools like a travel journal and the possibility to send your snapshots as e-postcards

TRAVEL TIPS

✈ A number of different major airlines such as British Airways *(www.british airways.com)* offer regular flights from the UK to Venice, from around £50 upwards, with prices averaging out at around £150 per person. Alitalia *(www.alitalia.com)* and several other international European airlines offer regular but not direct flights. Several no-frills airlines however do fly directly, e.g. easyJet *(www.easyjet.com)* and Ryanair *(www.ryanair.com)*, although not necessarily to Venice's main international airport. Some major carriers in the USA and Canada also offer direct flights as well as flights to major centres (Rome, London) and connecting flights to Venice. Venice's international Marco Polo Airport is on the northern border of the lagoon in Tessera *(http://airport-venice.com)*. Many cheaper flights are to Treviso airport located 20 km (12.5 miles) inland *(www. trevisoairport.it)*.

RESPONSIBLE TRAVEL

It doesn't take a lot to be environmentally friendly whilst travelling. Don't just think about your carbon footprint whilst flying to and from your holiday destination but also about how you can protect nature and culture abroad. As a tourist it is especially important to respect nature, look out for local products, cycle instead of driving, save water and much more. If you would like to find out more about eco-tourism please visit: *www.ecotourism.org*

GETTING INTO VENICE

From Treviso airport, the Eurobus "Canova" offers a shuttle service by way of Mestre (single fare 10 euros, return 18 euros, in combination with a single or mutliple day ticket only 4/8 euros, tickets at the terminal). From Venice's international Marco Polo Airport, the *Alilaguna* line *vaporetti* travel from the airport to the old town, Murano and the Lido *(8–15 euros depending on destination, reduced rates if booked online | travel time around 1 hour | www.alilaguna.it)*; alternatively, you can take one of the extremely expensive taxi boats *(motoscafi)*. There is a scheduled bus service *(www.atvo.it)* every 30 minutes between the airport and Piazzale Roma; fare (line 5): 6 euros, reduced fare in combination with a single or multiple day ticket.

🚗 Venice is reached by car over the Ponte della Libertà causeway. We recommend that day visitors park in one of the – quite expensive and often full – multi-storey car parks near the old town around the Piazzale Roma or on Tronchetto Island. Both have recently been connected by a "people mover", an almost 900 m-long cable car on stilts (ticket: 1.30 euros). The car parks on the mainland in Fusina, Treporti and Punta Sabbioni are less expensive. A modern tram line, opened in 2015, now connects Mestre and Venice via the Ponte della Libertà.

🚆 Venice can easily be reached by train from major cities all over Europe. But if you really want something different, try the Venice Simplon Orient Express *(www.belmond.com)*. It is a privately-run train of historic and beautifully-restored

From arrival to weather

Holiday from start to finish: the most important addresses and information for your Venice trip

1920s, 30s & 50s coaches, providing a classic luxury train experience between London, Paris, Innsbruck and Venice. It links London and Venice roughly once a week between March and November, the complete journey taking 24 hours and costing around 2,500 euros per person one way.

BANKS & MONEY

There are a great number of cash dispensers throughout the city and major credit cards are accepted almost everywhere.

CALENDAR OF EVENTS

The best way to find out about events, etc. is through the daily newspapers *Il Gazzettino* and *La Nuova Venezia* and the (Italian/English) pamphlets *Venezia News, Un Ospite di Venezia, Venezia da Vivere* and *Meeting Venice*. The last two are available free of charge at all arrival points, in hotel receptions, travel offices, etc.

CITY PASS VENEZIA UNICA

This personalized card is the cheapest way to take advantage of the public services in Venice. It is valid for seven days, making it easy for visitors to pick and choose their own agendas. It includes free admission to attractions such as the Doge's Palace, a variety of churches and the public museums plus discounts for other cultural sites. Bookable extras include tickets for public transportation, parking garages, public toilets and access to the city's WiFi network. The basic version costs 39.90 euros for adults over 30 and 29,90 euros for those ages 6 to 29. The pass can be purchased online *(www.veneziaunica.it)* or at the va-

BUDGETING

Vaporetto	7 euros *for a single ticket*
Gondola	80 euros *for a 30-minute trip*
Snack	from 3 euros *for a panino at the bar*
Entrance	3 euros *for entrance to one of the major churches*
Wine	from 1.60 euros *for a small glass of white wine at the bar*
Espresso	1–2 euros *for a cup at the bar*

poretti stops Tronchetto, Piazzale Roma, Rialto, Lido, Burano and Punta Sabbioni.

CUSTOMS

EU citizens can import and export goods for their personal use tax free (e.g. 800 cigarettes, 10 L of spirits over 22%). Visitors from other countries must observe the following limits, except for items for personal use. Duty free are: max 50 g perfume, 200 cigarettes, 50 cigars, 250 g tabacco, 1 L spirits (over 22 % vol) and 2 L of any wine.

EMBASSIES & CONSULATES

BRITISH CONSULATE
Piazzale Donatori di Sangue 2/5 | 30171 Venice-Mestre | tel. (39) 041 505 5990 | http://ukinitaly.fco.gov.uk/en/

EMBASSY OF THE UNITED STATES

Consular Agency (at Venice Marco Polo Airport) | General Aviation Terminal | Viale Galileo Galilei 30 – 30173 Tessera (VE) | tel. (39) 041 541 5944 | http://milan.usconsulate.gov/about-us/consular-agency-venice.html

EMERGENCY SERVICES

Emergency: *tel. 112* | Police: *tel. 113* | fire brigade: *tel. 115* | ambulance *tel. 118*

GONDOLAS

For many people, a romantic ● ride in a gondola is one of the highlights of a visit to Venice. 30 minutes for up to six people costs 80 euros during the day and 100 euros at night (extensions cost 40 and 50 euros respectively for 20 minutes). The gondolieri wait for their passengers at the Piazzetta San Marco, in front of the Hotel Danieli, behind St Mark's Square in the Bacino Orseolo, as well as along the Canal Grande at the Piazzale Roma, near the railway station at Campo Santa Sofia, by Rialto Bridge and the San Tomà, Giglio and Vallaresso *vaporetto* stops.

There are gondola ferries, so-called *traghetti*, that carry passengers across the Canal Grande for 2 euros per crossing at San Marcuola, near Santa Sofia next to the Ca' d'Oro, at the Riva del Carbon next to Rialto Bridge, near San Tomà, between San Samuele and Ca' Rezzonico, as well as by Santa Maria del Giglio.

GUIDED TOURS

You can book officially authorised, English-speaking guides from the *Cooperativa Guide Turistiche (tel. 04 15 20 90 38 | ww.guidevenezia.it)*. The price for a personal tour lasting two hours is 137 euros.

HEALTH

The EHIC, the EU insurance card issued by the British authorities, is valid in Italy. It is recommended that you take out travel healthcare insurance to cover the costs of private treatment. The consulate will help you find an English-speaking doctor. In emergencies, the Santi Giovanni e Paolo Hospital can be reached under *tel. 04 15 29 41 11*, the health centre on the Lido under *tel. 04 12 38 56 68*. The *pronto soccorso* section is responsible for emergency admission. Information on chemist's open outside of the regular hours is posted or available from the telephone information service at *tel. 192*.

HIGH WATER

Acqua alta is almost part of everyday Venetian life in the winter. If there is the threat of flooding, warning sirens are sounded throughout the entire city. The nightmare usually lasts for a few hours. There are maps in some *vaporetto* stops showing where there are wooden bridges that make it possible to reach your destination without getting your feet wet – even when the city is under water. The water-level forecast can be found on the internet under *www.comune.venezia.it/maree*.

INFORMATION IN ADVANCE

www.turismovenezia.it is the official website of the tourism association, *www.comune.venezia.it* the digital visiting card of the city administration with many useful links. The official tourist website of the city with detailed instructions on how to purchase the city pass (see p. 110) as well as information about local attractions and events is *www.veneziaunica.it*. Information on public transportation routes, timetables and tariffs is available under *www.actv.it*; there is a detailed description of the eleven city museums at *www.visitmuve.it*. Information, in Italian and English, on art, sporting and other events, can also be found at *www.aguestinvenice.com* and *www.meeting-venice.it*. *www.veniceonline.it* provides a helpful overview with many links ranging from hotel bookings to the weather forecast and programme of events.

INFORMATION IN VENICE

The central contact address by phone is the *Tourist Contact Center (daily 9am–7pm | tel. 04 15 29 87 11)*. The most important contact point in town ist the information office at the south-west corner of St Mark's Square under the arcade *(daily 8:30am–7pm)*. The other *uffici informazioni* that are open throughout the year are at Piazzale Roma *(daily 8:30am–2pm)*, at the railway station *(daily 8:30am–7pm)*, the Marco Polo Airport *(daily 9am–8pm)* and

in Punta Sabbioni *(daily 8:30am–7pm, in the winter only am)*.

Central information office of the Tourism association (not open to the public): *Azienda di Promozione Turistica APT (Palazzetto Carmagnani | Fondamenta Cornér-Zaguri 2637 | 30124 Venezia | www.turismovenezia.it)*

Tickets for scheduled *vaporetto* services and city buses, as well as for theatre performances and other events, are available at the counters of the *Vela* enterprise (Piazzale Roma, Santa Lucia railway station, Lido, Tronchetto and other locations). In addition, you can obtain all kinds of information, as well as reservations and bookings for many events under *www.veneziaunica.it* or tel. *0 41 24 24* (in Italian and English).

Complaints about unsatisfactory public services or improper treatment of tourists can be submitted via e-mail to complaint. apt@turismovenezia.it. During its normal business hours, the tourism association APT also offers assistance under tel. 04 15 29 87 26.

KEEP FIT!

Why not learn to do what the gondolieri do? Two traditional rowing clubs, *Società Canottieri Bucintoro (tel. 04 15 20 56 30 | www.bucintoro.org)* and *Associazione Canottieri Giudecca (tel. 04 15 28 74 09 | www.canottierigiudecca.com)* give short courses where even beginners can learn how to steer a *sandolo*, a *mascareta* or *gondola* elegantly over the water and through the canals. A few hours of cycling along the seashore can be wonderful alternative to the many, many hours spent wandering

through the city. Bicycles can be rented at the Lido vaporetto stop: *Gardin* on *Piazza Santa Maria Elisabetta 2 (tel. 04 12 76 00 05 | www.biciclettegardin. com)* and *Renato Scarpi (tel. 04 15 2 62 80 19 | www.lidoonbike.it)* at *Viale Santa Maria Elisabetta 21b*. From there, you pedal off towards the south as far as the picturesque villages Malamocco and Alberoni, and if you feel like and are fit enough, ride past the Lido di Pellestrina along the stone causeways *(murazzi)* to the small fishing town of Chioggia.

INTERNET ACCESS & WI-FI

It possible for you to log in to the WiFi network and access the internet near St Mark's Square, free of charge. The only condition is that you purchase a museum ticket or pass online under *www.venez iaunica.it*. Most hotels now offer either a computer with Internet for guest use or provide WiFi access (password protected) for smartphones, tablets or laptops.

PHONES & MOBILE PHONES

The country code for Italy is 0039 (UK 0044, US 001, Ireland 00353) followed by the number of the person you are calling, including the first 0. There are no problems with mobile phone reception and with an Italian prepaid card you can avoid the

costs for incoming calls. Local and long-distance calls are cheapest from telephone booths. Phone cards *(carta telefonica)* are available for 5 or 10 euros in post offices, bars, *tabacchi* or newsstands.

PORTERS

These helpers are sometimes extremely useful in this city of bridges and narrow streets. They can be found at the railway station, Piazzale Roma, by the Accademia, near San Marco and the Hotel Danieli. The price for transporting each piece of luggage within the old town is 24 euros.

POSTAGE

Stamps *(francobolli)* can be bought in post offices or tobacconist's shops.

WEATHER IN VENICE

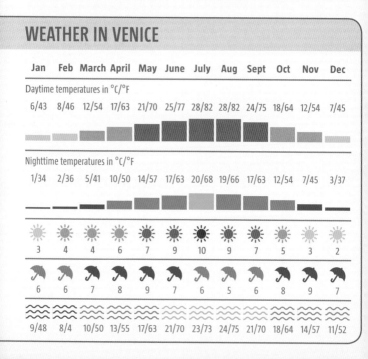

	Jan	Feb	March	April	May	June	July	Aug	Sept	Oct	Nov	Dec
Daytime temperatures in °C/°F	6/43	8/46	12/54	17/63	21/70	25/77	28/82	28/82	24/75	18/64	12/54	7/45
Nighttime temperatures in °C/°F	1/34	2/36	5/41	10/50	14/57	17/63	20/68	19/66	17/63	12/54	7/45	3/37
☀ Sunshine hours/day	3	4	4	6	7	9	10	9	7	5	3	2
☂ Precipitation days/month	6	6	7	8	9	7	6	5	6	8	9	7
≈ Water temperature in °C/°F	9/48	8/4	10/50	13/55	17/63	21/70	23/73	24/75	21/70	18/64	14/57	11/52

Postage for postcards and standard letters to EU countries and Switzerland is 95 cents.

PUBLIC TRANSPORT

The most convenient way to get around in Venice is by using the scheduled boat services *(vaporetti)* operated by the city's transport authority ACTV *(www.actv.it)*. There are 24 lines serving the Canal Grande, the most important side canals and also connecting the old town with the Lido, the islands in the lagoon and the mainland. A single ticket costs a hefty 7 euros, a 24 hour ticket 20 euros; there are also tickets for 2, 3 and 7 days at a price of 30, 40 and 60 euros respectively. The normal operating times for the *vaporetti* vary depending on the line, but most begin between 5am and 7am and end between 8pm and 1am. Night-owls take note: *linee notturni* boats run all night long along the Canal Grande and the Giudecca canal as well as to Lido and the northern lagoon islands.

TAXIS

The water taxis, so-called *motoscafi (www. motoscafivenezia.it),* are a rather expensive proposition and are most suitable for small groups (up to a maximum of 10 people). Additional charges are made for more than 2 passengers, trips at night, telephone bookings *(04 15 22 23 03),* large pieces of luggage, etc. The most important stops are at the Piazzale Roma, the railway station, near Rialto Bridge, in San Marco, at the Lido and the airport.

TIPPING

A service charge is normally included, but waiters, hotel maids, gondolieri etc. are naturally pleased if you reward them for friendly service. Five to ten percent is usual in restaurants.

WEATHER, WHEN TO GO

Venice has a moderate, Mediterranean climate. The hot sirocco wind blowing from Africa and the high humidity level can make it rather sticky in summer; the humidity is still there in winter when Venice can be cold and damp and, sometimes, foggy. From the climatic point of view, the best times to visit La Serenissima are April/May and September/October but some weeks in winter, when the air is crystal clear, have a very special charm. The weather on the web: *www.tempoitalia.it*

CURRENCY CONVERTER

£	€	€	£
1	1.40	1	0.72
3	4.17	3	2.15
5	6.96	5	3.59
13	18.08	13	9.34
40	55.65	40	28.75
75	104	75	53.89
120	167	120	86
250	348	250	180
500	696	500	359

$	€	€	$
1	0.92	1	1.09
3	2.75	3	3.27
5	4.58	5	5.45
13	11.92	13	14.18
40	36.67	40	43.64
75	69	75	81.82
120	110	120	131
250	229	250	273
500	458	500	545

For current exchange rates see www.xe.com

USEFUL PHRASES ITALIAN

PRONUNCIATION

c, cc	before e or i like ch in "church", e.g. ciabatta, otherwise like k
ch, cch	like k, e.g. pacchi, che
g, gg	before e or i like j in "just", e.g. gente, otherwise like g in "get"
gl	like "lli" in "million", e.g. figlio
gn	as in "cognac", e.g. bagno
sc	before e or i like sh, e.g. uscita
sch	like sk in "skill", e.g. Ischia
z	at the beginning of a word like dz in "adze", otherwise like ts

An accent on an Italian word shows that the stress is on the last syllable.
In other cases we have shown which syllable is stressed by placing a dot below the relevant vowel.

IN BRIEF

Yes/No/Maybe	Sì/No/Forse
Please/Thank you	Per favore/Grazie
Excuse me, please!	Scusa!/Mi scusi
May I...?/Pardon?	Posso...? / Come dice?/Prego?
I would like to.../Have you got...?	Vorrei.../Avete...?
How much is...?	Quanto costa...?
I (don't) like that	(Non) mi piace
good/bad	buono/cattivo/bene/male
broken/doesn't work	guasto/non funziona
too much/much/little/all/nothing	troppo/molto/poco/ tutto/niente
Help!/Attention!/Caution!	aiuto!/attenzione!/prudenza!
ambulance/police/fire brigade	ambulanza/polizia/vigili del fuoco
Prohibition/forbidden/danger/dangerous	divieto/vietato/pericolo/pericoloso
May I take a photo here/of you?	Posso fotografar La?

GREETINGS, FAREWELL

Good morning!/afternoon!/ evening!/night!	Buon giorno!/Buon giorno!/ Buona sera!/Buona notte!
Hello! / Goodbye!/See you	Ciao!/Salve! / Arrivederci!/Ciao!
My name is...	Mi chiamo...
What's your name?	Come si chiama?/Come ti chiami
I'm from...	Vengo da...

Parli italiano?

"Do you speak Italian?" This guide will help you to say the basic words and phrases in Italian.

DATE & TIME

Monday/Tuesday/Wednesday	lunedì/martedì/mercoledì
Thursday/Friday/Saturday	giovedì/venerdì/sabato
Sunday/holiday/ working day	domenica/(giorno) festivo/ (giorno) feriale
today/tomorrow/yesterday	oggi/domani/ieri
hour/minute	ora/minuto
day/night/week/month/year	giorno/notte/settimana/mese/anno
What time is it?	Che ora è? Che ore sono?
It's three o'clock/It's half past three	Sono le tre/Sono le tre e mezza
a quarter to four	le quattro meno un quarto/ un quarto alle quattro

TRAVEL

open/closed	aperto/chiuso
entrance/exit	entrata/uscita
departure/arrival	partenza/arrivo
toilets/ladies/gentlemen	bagno/toilette/signore/signori
(no) drinking water	acqua (non) potabile
Where is...?/Where are...?	Dov'è...?/Dove sono...?
left/right/straight ahead/back	sinistra/destra/dritto/indietro
close/far	vicino/lontano
bus/tram	bus/tram
taxi/cab	taxi/tassì
bus stop/cab stand	fermata/posteggio taxi
parking lot/parking garage	parcheggio/parcheggio coperto
street map/map	pianta/mappa
train station/harbour	stazione/porto
airport	aeroporto
schedule/ticket	orario/biglietto
supplement	supplemento
single/return	solo andata/andata e ritorno
train/track	treno/binario
platform	banchina/binario
I would like to rent...	Vorrei noleggiare...
a car/a bicycle	una macchina/una bicicletta
a boat	una barca
petrol/gas station	distributore/stazione di servizio
petrol/gas / diesel	benzina/diesel/gasolio
breakdown/repair shop	guasto/officina

FOOD & DRINK

Could you please book a table for tonight for four?	Vorrei prenotare per stasera un tavolo per quattro?
on the terrace/by the window	sulla terrazza/ vicino alla finestra
The menu, please/	La carta/il menù, per favore
Could I please have...?	Potrei avere...?
bottle/carafe/glass	bottiglia/caraffa/bicchiere
knife/fork/spoon/salt/pepper	coltello/forchetta/cucchiaio/sale/pepe
sugar/vinegar/oil/milk/cream/lemon	zucchero/aceto/olio/latte/panna/limone
cold/too salty/not cooked	freddo/troppo salato/non cotto
with/without ice/sparkling	con/senza ghiaccio/gas
vegetarian/allergy	vegetariano/vegetariana/allergia
May I have the bill, please?	Vorrei pagare/Il conto, per favore
bill/tip	conto/mancia

SHOPPING

Where can I find...?	Dove posso trovare...?
I'd like.../I'm looking for...	Vorrei.../Cerco...
Do you put photos onto CD?	Vorrei masterizzare delle foto su CD?
pharmacy/shopping centre/kiosk	farmacia/centro commerciale/edicola
department store/supermarket	grandemagazzino/supermercato
baker/market/grocery	forno/ mercato/negozio alimentare
photographic items/newspaper shop/	articoli per foto/giornalaio
100 grammes/1 kilo	un etto/un chilo
expensive/cheap/price/more/less	caro/economico/prezzo/di più/di meno
organically grown	di agricoltura biologica

ACCOMMODATION

I have booked a room	Ho prenotato una camera
Do you have any... left?	Avete ancora...
single room/double room	una (camera) singola/doppia
breakfast/half board/	prima colazione/mezza pensione/
full board (American plan)	pensione completa
at the front/seafront/lakefront	con vista/con vista sul mare/lago
shower/sit-down bath/balcony/terrace	doccia/bagno/balcone/terrazza
key/room card	chiave/scheda magnetica
luggage/suitcase/bag	bagaglio/valigia/borsa

BANKS, MONEY & CREDIT CARDS

bank/ATM/pin code	banca/bancomat/ codice segreto
cash/credit card	in contanti/carta di credito
bill/coin/change	banconota/moneta/il resto

HEALTH

doctor/dentist/paediatrician	medico/dentista/pediatra
hospital/emergency clinic	ospedale/pronto soccorso/guardia medica
fever/pain/inflamed/injured	febbre/dolori/infiammato/ferito
diarrhoea/nausea/sunburn	diarrea/nausea/scottatura solare
plaster/bandage/ointment/cream	cerotto/fasciatura/pomata/crema
pain reliever/tablet/suppository	antidolorifico/compressa/supposta

POST, TELECOMMUNICATIONS & MEDIA

stamp/letter/postcard	francobollo/lettera/cartolina
I need a landline phone card/ I'm looking for a prepaid card for my mobile	Mi serve una scheda telefonica per la rete fissa/Cerco una scheda prepagata per il mio cellulare
Where can I find internet access?	Dove trovo un accesso internet?
dial/connection/engaged	comporre/linea/occupato
socket/adapter/charger	presa/riduttore/caricabatterie
computer/battery/rechargeable battery	computer/batteria/accumulatore
internet address (URL)/e-mail address	indirizzo internet/indirizzo email
internet connection/wifi	collegamento internet/wi-fi
e-mail/file/print	email/file/stampare

LEISURE, SPORTS & BEACH

beach/bathing beach	spiaggia/bagno/stabilimento balneare
sunshade/lounger/cable car/chair lift	ombrellone/sdraio/funivia/seggiovia
(rescue) hut/avalanche	rifugio/valanga

NUMBERS

0	zero	15	quindici
1	uno	16	sedici
2	due	17	diciassette
3	tre	18	diciotto
4	quattro	19	diciannove
5	cinque	20	venti
6	sei	21	ventuno
7	sette	50	cinquanta
8	otto	100	cento
9	nove	200	duecento
10	dieci	1000	mille
11	undici	2000	duemila
12	dodici	10000	diecimila
13	tredici	½	un mezzo
14	quattordici	¼	un quarto

STREET ATLAS

Photo: St Mark's Campanile and Marciana library

Exploring Venice

The map on the back cover shows how the area has been sub-divided

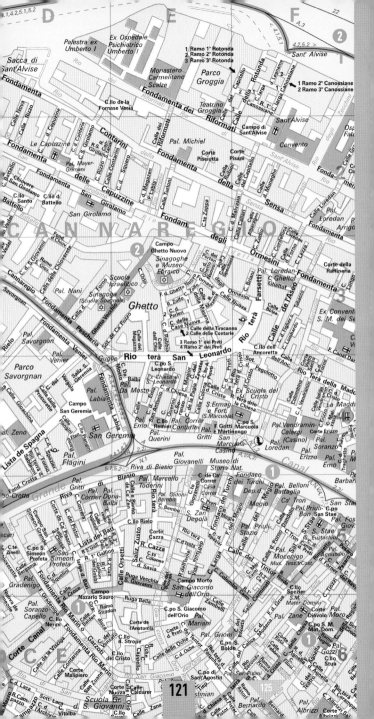

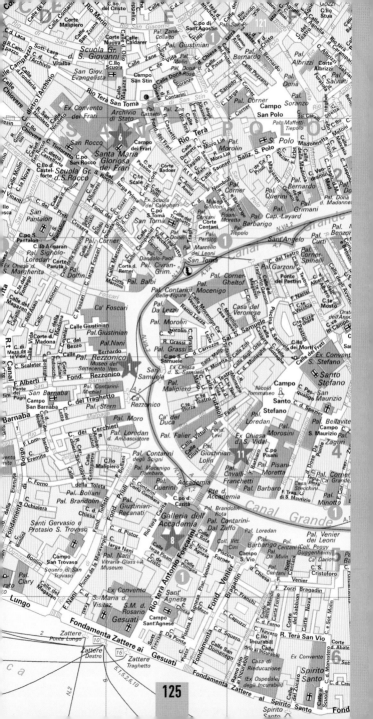

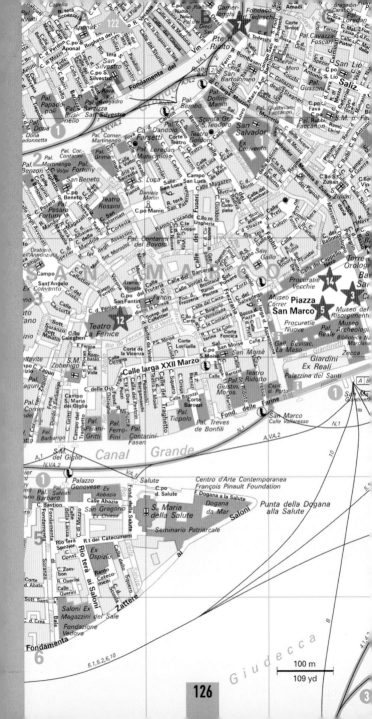

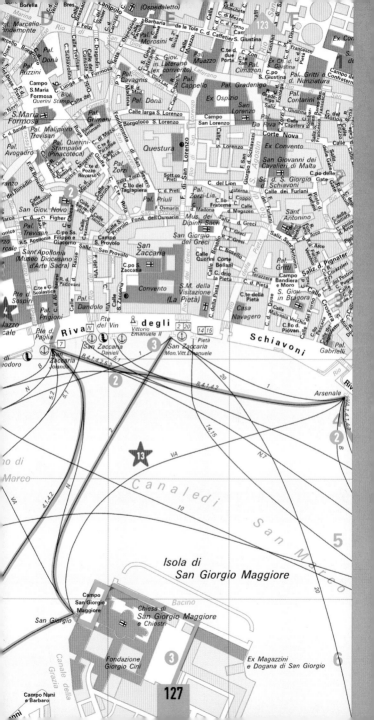

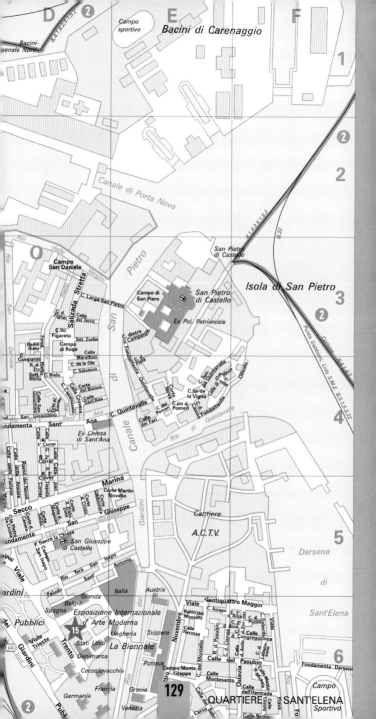

Bacini di Carenaggio

D · E · F

Campo sportivo

Bacini-senale Nord

Canale di Porta Nova

San Pietro di Castello

Isola di San Pietro

Campo San Daniele

Rio delle Gorne

Salizada Stretta

Larga San Pietro
C. d. Figher
Calle del Terco
C.llo Figareto
Sot. Zurlin
Campo di Ruga
Calle Marattoni
C. de le Ole
C. Salomon
Corte del Bianco
Calle Sant'Ana
Ramo Rielo
R. d. Zio
C. Campanati
Sott. P. C. Rielo
Stella
Calle Crosera
C. Canizzando

Campo di San Piero
San Pietro di Castello
Ex Pal. Patriarcale
C. dietro il Campanile
Fondamenta Quintavalle
C. Pietà
C. de la Mona
C.llo Quintavalle
Calle de la Valle
Olivolo
Punta Sabbioni, Lido S.M.E. B.51,52,22
Canale
di
San Daniele

Corte Nova
C.llo de la Vigna
C. del Pomeri
C.po d. Pomeri
C. Fondamenta

San Gioacchino
Sant' Ana
C. Quintavalle
Calle del Fari
Rio di Quintavalle

Ex Chiesa di Sant'Ana

Calle delle Furlane
R. 1° Correr
R. 2° Correr
Calle delle Ancore
Ramo del Nicoli
R. 3° Correr
Calle delle Furlane

Marina
Corte Martin Novello
Corte Sabbionera
Corte Colonne

Secco
Corte d.
Corte d. Genoa
Fondamenta

Corte Nova
Corte di Zorzi
San Giuseppe

San Giuseppe di Castello
F. fianco la Chiesa
Campo San Piero

Rio Terà San Isepo
Sant' Antonio

Paludo
Sant'

Cantiere
A.C.T.V.

Darsena

di

Sant'Elena

Giardini
Pubblici

Viale Trieste
Viale Trento

Olanda
Belgio
Spagna
Italia
Austria

Ramo del Montello
Viale Ventiquattro Maggio
C. Asiago
C. d. Arco
C. d. Pozzoleon
C. d. Arco
Calle del Forno
C. d. Congregazione
Calle Nervesa
C. d. Asiago
C. d. Labia
C. Congregazione
Calle Podgora

Esposizione Internazionale d'Arte Moderna
Ungheria
Svizzera
Novembre
R. d. Pasubio
C. d. Montello
Calle d. Asilo
Calle del Pasubio

15

Stati Uniti
Danimarca

La Biennale

Cecoslovacchia
Polonia
Campo Monte Grappa
Calle Montesanto
Calle Oslavia

Francia
Grecia

129

Germania
Venezia

Fondamenta Darsena

Campo

QUARTIERE SANT'ELENA
Sportivo

Giardini
Viale del
VA

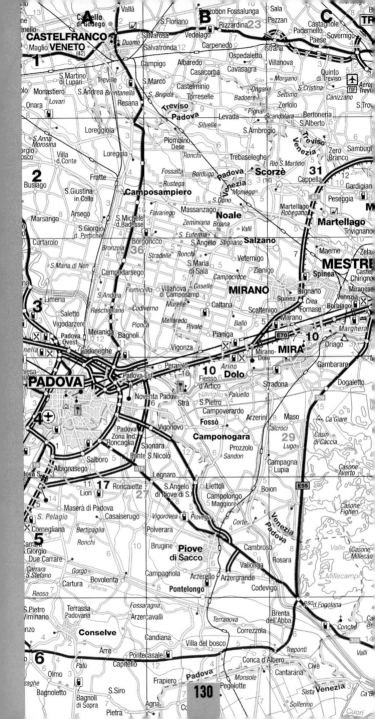

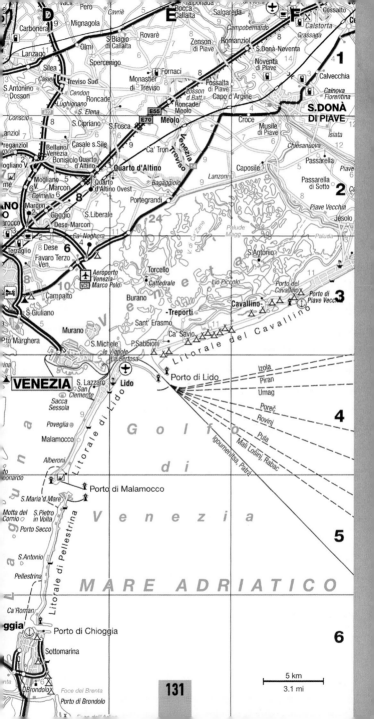

This index lists a selection of the streets and squares shown in the street atlas.

KEY TO STREET ATLAS

Strada a quattro corsie Vierspurige Straße		Road with four lanes Route à quatre voies
Strada di attraversamento Durchgangsstraße		Thoroughfare Route de transit
Strada principale Hauptstraße		Main road Route principale
Altre strade Sonstige Straßen		Other roads Autres routes
Parcheggio Parkplatz	P	Parking place Parking
Informazioni Information	i	Information Information
Ferrovia principale con stazione Hauptbahn mit Bahnhof		Main railway with station Chemin de fer principal avec gare
Altra ferrovia Sonstige Bahn		Other railway Autre ligne
Traghetto per automobili Autofähre		Car ferry Bac pour automobiles
Traghetto per persone (Vaporetto) Personenfähre (Vaporetto)		Passenger ferry (Vaporetto) Bac pour piétons (Vaporetto)
Pontile per le gondole - Stazione terminale Gondelanlegestelle - Endhaltestelle		Landing stage for gondolas - Terminus Embarcadère pour les gondoles - Terminus
Chiesa interessante - Altre chiesa Sehenswerte Kirche - Sonstige Kirche		Church of interest - Other church Église remarquable - Autre église
Sinagoga Synagoge		Synagogue Synagogue
Posto di polizia - Ufficio postale Polizeistation - Postamt		Police station - Post office Poste de police - Bureau de poste
Ostello della gioventù - Ospedale Jugendherberge - Krankenhaus		Youth hostel - Hospital Auberge de jeunesse - Hôpital
Monumento - Faro Denkmal - Leuchtturm		Monument - Lighthouse Monument - Phare
Caseggiato, edificio pubblico Bebaute Fläche, öffentliches Gebäude		Built-up area, public building Zone bâtie, bâtiment public
Zona industriale Industriegelände		Industrial area Zone industrielle
Parco, bosco Park, Wald		Park, forest Parc, bois
Cimitero Friedhof		Cemetery Cimetière
Cimitero ebraico Jüdischer Friedhof		Jewish cemetery Cimetière juif
MARCO POLO Giro avventura 1 MARCO POLO Erlebnistour 1		MARCO POLO Discovery Tour 1 MARCO POLO Tour d'aventure 1
MARCO POLO Giro avventura MARCO POLO Erlebnistouren		MARCO POLO Discovery Tours MARCO POLO Tours d'aventure
MARCO POLO Highlight		MARCO POLO Highlight

MARCO POLO TRAVEL GUIDES

The travel guides with
Insider
Tips

INDEX

This index lists all sights, museums and places featured in this guide. Numbers in bold indicate a main entry.

WRITE TO US

e-mail: info@marcopologuides.co.uk

Did you have a great holiday?
Is there something on your mind?
Whatever it is, let us know!
Whether you want to praise, alert us
to errors or give us a personal tip –
MARCO POLO would be pleased to
hear from you.
We do everything we can to provide the
very latest information for your trip.

Nevertheless, despite all of our authors'
thorough research, errors can creep in.
MARCO POLO does not accept any
liability for this. Please contact us by
e-mail or post.

MARCO POLO Travel Publishing Ltd
Pinewood, Chineham Business Park
Crockford Lane, Chineham
Basingstoke, Hampshire RG24 8AL
United Kingdom

PICTURE CREDITS
Cover photograph: Canal Grande and Rialto Bridge (Getty Images/Photographer's Choice RF: Child)
Photos: Carlo & Giorgio (18 bottom); DuMont Bildarchiv: S. Lubenow (76/77, 106 bottom); R. Freyer (105); GALLERIA D'ARTE L'OCCHIO (18 top); Getty Images: S. Blanco (99), Maremagnum (90/91), M. Secchi (6); Getty Images/Photographer's Choice RF: Child (1); R. Hackenberg (51); huber-images: Baviera (40, 43), M. Carassale (62), Cozzi (10), L. Da Ros (53), Fantuz (68 left, 81), Fischer (20/21), Gräfenhain (42), J. Huber (5, 34), Mirau (12/13, 49), M. Rellini (37), G. Simeone (flap left, 104); huber-images/PictureFinders (103); © iStockphoto: Lynn Seeden (19 top); Laif: Bungert (74), Celentano (84), Degiorgis (19 bottom), N. Hilger (46), Kirchgessner (8), H. Kloever (70/71), Zinn (55); Laif/Aurora: Renck (104/105); Laif/Contrasto: Bossan (59), Savino (78); Laif/Invision: Dinulescu (33); Laif/Palladium: Burg + Schuh (31); laif/Polaris: M. Silvestri (flap right); laif/Zurita: dePablo (4 top, 17); Look: J. Greune (11), K. Jaeger (95, 118/119), K. Johaentges (14/15, 100/101), S. Lubenow (67), K. Wothe (26/27); look/age fotostock (2/3); mauritius images: J. Warburton-Lee (4 bottom, 60/61, 102); mauritius images/age (7, 9, 56); mauritius images/Alamy (82/83); mauritius images/CuboImages (64, 72, 89); mauritius images/imagebroker: S. Lubenow (68 right); mauritius images/United Archives (102/103); Schapowalow/SIME: M. Carassale (25), L. Da Ros (38/39); T. Stankiewicz (23, 106 top, 107); Venice Kayak: René Seindal (18 centre)

2ⁿᵈ Edition – fully revised and updated 2016
Worldwide Distribution: Marco Polo Travel Publishing Ltd, Pinewood, Chineham Business Park, Crockford Lane, Basingstoke, Hampshire RG24 8AL, United Kingdom. Email: sales@marcopolouk.com
© MAIRDUMONT GmbH & Co. KG, Ostfildern
Chief editor: Marion Zorn
Author: Walter M. Weiss; Editor: Nikolai Michaelis
Programme supervision: Susanne Heimburger, Tamara Hub, Nikolai Michaelis, Kristin Schimpf, Martin Silbermann
Picture editors: Gabriele Forst, Anja Schlatterer; What's hot: wunder media, Munich
Cartography street atlas and pull-out map: © MAIRDUMONT, Ostfildern
Design: milchhof : atelier, Berlin; front cover, pull-out map cover, page 1: factor product munich; Discovery Tours: Susan Chaaban, Dipl.-Des. (FH)
Translated from German by Robert McInnes, Jennifer Walcoff Neuheiser; editor of the English edition: Christopher Wynne
Prepress: InterMedia, Ratingen; writehouse, Cologne
Phrase book in cooperation with Ernst Klett Sprachen GmbH, Stuttgart, Editorial by Pons Wörterbücher

MIX
Paper from responsible sources
FSC® C124385
www.fsc.org

DOS & DON'TS 👆

A few things you should bear in mind in Venice

DON'T TAKE YOUR SHIRT OFF WHEN WALKING AROUND THE OLD CITY

No matter how hot its, bare male or over-exposed female torsos or beachwear are taboo on the streets of the *centro storico*. And going into a church in that kind of getup is even more frowned upon.

DON'T ORDER PASTA AS A MAIN COURSE

It might be all right to fill up on a plate of pasta in a cheaper restaurant or tourist trap and then simply pay and go. In better-class restaurants, however, there is an unwritten law forbidding this. Here, as everywhere else in Italy, pasta is a *primo piatto* and is followed by a main course of meat or fish. If you need a snack, a sandwich – a *panino* – or a couple of *tramezzini* at the bar are a better idea.

DON'T GET TAKEN IN BY FALSE TRAFFIC WARDENS

So-called *abusivi*, illegal traffic wardens, get up to no good around the car parks on Tronchetto Island. Sometimes dressed in orange jackets, sometimes in white shirts, white-and-blue caps and armbands, they look almost like the real thing and attempt to manoeuvre unsuspecting newcomers to the taxi boats of a private shuttle service. This will make the trip to San Marco much, much more expensive than by *vaporetto*.

Another popular "service" is a to Murano. After the obligatory visit a glassblower's workshop, you will ha to pay for the ride back yourself – spite of what you were promised.

DON'T PICNIC ON THE PIAZZA

An ever-increasing number of tourists have started taking a break on and near St Mark's Square and this has caused the authorities to ban sitting, drinking and eating on the Piazza, its steps, in the arcades, or on the Piazzetta by the jetties. The Giardini ex Reali, 150 metres away, has officially been declared the place where you can tuck in to your food in peace.

DON'T DODGE FARES

You might well be tempted, but be careful! Inspections are sometimes made on board *vaporetti* and, if you get caught without a ticket, you will be fined at least 50 euros.

DON'T FEED THE PIGEONS

It was a photographic ritual for generations of tourists: feeding pigeons with specially-bought bird food. But now the authorities have finally had enough of the flocks of birds and all the dirt. Those who get caught feeding the pigeons will be fined 500 euros. And street salesmen are not allowed to sell food for our feathered friends either.